D1625915

TALES OF A TILLER GIRL

At just four years old, Irene Holland knew
there was only one thing to do with her life:
dance. There was a whole host of obstacles in
her way – her height, injuries and her
widowed mother unable to afford expensive
stage-school fees among them – but not even
the Blitz and a near-miss from a German
bomb would keep Rene out of her dancing
shoes. At eighteen, she was accepted into the
world-famous, high-kicking dancing troupe
the Tiller Girls, and with it came adventures
she'd never imagined...

TALES OF A TILLER GIRL

TALES OF A TILLER GIRL

by

Irene Holland

Magna Large Print Books
Long Preston, North Yorkshire,
BD23 4ND, England.

British Library Cataloguing in Publication Data.

Holland, Irene
        Tales of a Tiller Girl.

        A catalogue record of this book is
        available from the British Library

        ISBN   978-0-7505-4092-6

First published in Great Britain by HarperElement
An imprint of HarperCollins*Publishers* 2014

Copyright © Irene Holland 2014

Cover illustration by arrangement with mirrorpix

Irene Holland asserts the moral right to be identified as the
author of this work

Published in Large Print 2015 by arrangement with
HarperCollins Publishers

Magna Large Print is an imprint of Library Magna Books Ltd.

Printed and bound in Great Britain by
T.J. (International) Ltd., Cornwall, PL28 8RW

This book is a work of non-fiction based
on the experiences of the author. In some
cases the names of people, places and
details of events have been changed
for legal reasons or to protect
the privacy of others.

Plate section is courtesy of the author.

For my lovely mum Kitty,
who inspired me to achieve my dream.

And to my children, grandchildren and
great-grandchildren, in the hope that
you all find your passion in life,
as I have in dancing.

Contents

1

On Our Own

The little girl walked down the hospital ward tightly clutching her mother's hand. Nurses bustled up and down in their starched white uniforms and capes, and the smell of carbolic soap was overpowering. Finally they got to a bed at the end, which had the curtains drawn around it for privacy.

'Come here, dear,' said one of the nurses, lifting up the girl and sitting her on the bed so that she had a better view of the man lying in it.

He looked very thin and frail, and he had a nasty, hacking cough. Her mother passed the man a handkerchief, and as he patted his mouth the girl noticed bright red spots of blood splattered all over the white material.

Although just two years old, the child knew instinctively that it was serious. Maybe it was her mother's tears that gave it away or the pale, gaunt face of the man lying in the bed. Every breath he took was so laboured and shallow and seemed to require so much effort that it almost sounded like his last.

'Poor Daddy,' she sighed.

You see, that little girl was me, and that was my first, last and only memory of my father, Edwin Bott.

I was born in 1930 in a nursing home on the edge of Wandsworth Common in south-west London. My brother, Raymond, was eleven years older than me and, like a lot of children, I think I was what you'd call a bit of a mistake! I was from a very musical background – my father was a cellist and my mother, Kitty, was a professional violinist. They had met in the orchestra pit while they were playing music for the silent films when Mum was seventeen and my dad was seven years older. When they first got married they lived in Oxford, and that's where my brother was born, but then they moved up to London to play in the theatre orchestras. My father also used to play in a quartet on banana boats that would take passengers to Rio de Janeiro and bring bananas back. He would be away for weeks at a time, and the bananas he was given by the crew would be completely rotten by the time he got back home to London.

My name was Irene but everyone called me Rene. I was named after my father's half-sister Rene Gibbons. She was a Goldwyn Girl, part of a glamorous company of female dancers employed by the famous Hollywood producer Samuel Goldwyn in the Twenties and Thirties to perform in his films and musicals. Many female stars got their big break in his troupes, including Lucille Ball and Betty Grable. Although I'd never met her, I'd seen from a photograph she once sent us that Rene was an incredibly beautiful woman. She looked like something from a Pre-Raphaelite painting, with her long auburn hair and huge green eyes. Unfortunately she and Mum never got along, I suspect probably due to a little bit of jealousy on my mother's part, although she never really told me why.

'I wanted to call you Violet,' Mum used to say to me as I was growing up. 'But your sneaky father went off to the town hall one day and registered your birth without me knowing.

'When he came back and I saw the name Irene on your birth certificate there were a few fireworks, let me tell you.'

I could well imagine. My mother was only tiny but she had a sparky temper, that was for sure.

Sadly I was too young to remember Dad, apart from that one time when I had visited him in hospital. I was only two when he died of tuberculosis at the age of thirty-three. He had terrible asthma, so I think it affected him very quickly. It must have been horrible for my mother and Raymond to see him in so much pain as his lungs disintegrated and he constantly coughed up blood. There was

no cure in those days and it was highly infectious. My brother and I were tested for it,
but thankfully we were clear.

We'd always been comfortably off, but
after my father died we were left destitute.
My brother had to leave his private boarding school and it was a real struggle. Mum
had a small amount from her widow's pen-
sion so she decided to buy a 1920s house in
London. But we were there less than a year
as she couldn't keep up with the mortgage
payments. Eventually the house was repos-
sessed and she lost her deposit. There were
no Social Services then, and my mother
couldn't work because she had me and
she'd lost all her income from Dad.

'We're going to have to move in with your
grandmother and grandfather,' she told me.

I was three by then and this is where most
of my memories start. Her parents, Henry
and Kate Livermore, lived in a large, three-
storey Victorian terrace in Battersea, south-
west London. We called them Gaga and
Papa because my brother couldn't say their
names properly when he was little and those
nicknames just stuck.

The house seemed huge to me as Raymond and I tore around it. There was a big
sitting-room at the front with settees and an
open fire and all this lovely antique furniture. A passageway led to a tiny scullery
with a big copper pot with a fire underneath

where you would boil your washing and a really tired-looking porcelain sink. There were no hot-water taps in those days, of course. Then there was a dining-room with a big range cooker that had a coal fire underneath a couple of hot plates and took hours to heat up. On the second floor there was another living-room, two bedrooms and a bathroom, and on the very top floor was a tiny, dusty attic room.

'This is where we'll live, children,' Mum told me as we climbed up the steep staircase to the attic.

'Where's all the furniture, Mummy?' I asked.

It was very dark and shivery cold, and there was hardly anything in it. But there was a double bed for Mum and me to share, a camp bed for Raymond and a little larder where we could keep our food.

There was only one very dim electric light up there, and one night while we were sitting there it went out. I screamed, as I was so afraid of the dark.

'I'll go and find out what's happened,' said Mum.

She went downstairs to have a look while I sat there, completely petrified. A few minutes later she came storming up the stairs holding a candle. I could tell by the look on her face that she was fuming.

'I don't believe it,' she said. 'They've cut

us off.'

Mum hadn't been able to afford to pay her share of money for the meter that week, so my grandparents had cut off the electricity supply to the attic. From then on, even though the lights were blazing downstairs, we had to make do with a single candle. Mum was absolutely furious.

I was too young to really understand at the time, but now looking back, no wonder. How awful to do that to their own widowed daughter at a time when she so needed their help and support. I was old enough to know it wasn't nice, though.

'Why are Gaga and Papa being horrid to you?' I asked her.

'Your grandparents didn't like it when I married Daddy, as he believed in different things to them,' she explained.

My grandparents were right-wing Conservatives and extremely religious, which was the norm in those days, while my father was the complete opposite. He was a very left-wing socialist and an atheist. In fact, when he died he insisted that there was no funeral or flowers and he was buried in an unmarked grave somewhere in London. He used to speak at Speakers' Corner in Hyde Park and was one of the founder members of the Socialist Party of Great Britain. When he and my mother had gone off to the register office to get married in secret when she was

eighteen, Mum's family had practically dis-
owned her.

'But I loved your father and it doesn't
matter what they think,' said Mum, giving
me a kiss on the forehead.

I could see she was holding back the tears
but I never once saw her cry in front of me.
She was very loving, and was always kissing
and cuddling me. I think in a way she
needed me as much as I needed her.

My mother was a very proud person, so I
could tell it was humiliating for her to have
to go cap in hand to her parents and to have
absolutely nothing.

One morning she was busy cleaning and
tidying up our room.

'I'm getting everything spick and span as
the means test people are coming today,' she
told me.

I wasn't sure what exactly that meant, but
half an hour later a stern-looking woman in
a suit came up to the attic. She opened up
the larder door and had a good look inside.

'As you can see there's nothing in there,'
my mother told her frostily.

I could tell that Mum was very annoyed to
have to ask for help.

'What's that lady doing?' I said.

'She's checking to see how much food
we've got,' she told me. 'Or should I say how
little.'

I was even put out to work to try to hel

Mum make ends meet. I remember we were walking to the shop one day when a woman stopped my mother in the street.

'Oh, what a pretty little thing,' she said to me. 'Look at those great big brown eyes.'

I was such a show-off, and even as a toddler I knew how to play to a crowd. I opened my eyes even wider, fluttered my eyelashes and flashed her my best and biggest smile.

'I know a photographer looking for child models,' she told Mum. 'I'm sure he would love your daughter to pose for him.'

The photographer in question turned out to be a very famous man called Marcus Adams. He was a renowned children's photographer who had taken pictures of King George V's six children and all of the royal family. Although I couldn't have been more than three, I remember sitting there in his studio in a little woollen hat and jacket. I was paid three guineas a time, which was quite a lot in those days, and Mum was given copies of the shots, which were very beautiful, pale, sepia photographs printed on soft paper.

Things at home continued to be frosty between Mum and my grandparents. She was allowed downstairs to cook, but then she would always bring our food back up to the attic for us to eat at our little table. We'd never have a meal with them.

My mother was a good cook and we always 'ad lots of fresh vegetables to disguise the fact we couldn't afford much meat. We'd have our main meal of the day at lunchtime and she'd rustle up pies and stews, apple tarts and cakes. I liked having a boiled egg for tea, which she'd bring up to the attic for me on a silver tray.

Looking back, it was a very peculiar situation. Here were two opposing ideas of life – my mother's and my grandparents' – and then me in the middle seeing both sides of it. My grandparents were all right to me and Raymond, and I got on with my grandfather quite well. He used to be a French horn player in the Grenadier Guards, and one afternoon he started stomping up and down the hallway.

'Come on, Rene,' he bellowed. 'Let's pretend we're in the Grenadier Guards.'

I giggled as he marched up and down pretending that he was blowing his French horn.

'Come here and I'll tell you a story about when I was little,' he said.

He told me how he grew up in Devon with his father. He'd hated his stepmother, so he ran away from home at the age of fourteen and pretended he was sixteen so he could join the army. He'd never fought but had become a very good French horn player and afterwards had played in the pits in London orchestras.

'I played at Buckingham Palace for Queen

Victoria's birthday, you know,' he told me.

'You met the Queen?' I gasped. 'What was she like?'

'Oh, dreadful woman,' he grumbled.

'Why's that, Papa?'

'She used to come out on the balcony all in black after her husband had died, and even if it was pouring with rain we'd have to stand there and play for hours. Sometimes she wouldn't even bother coming out and would just have a quick look out of her bedroom window.'

He also described how he'd played for two very famous dancers, Anna Pavlova and Isadora Duncan.

'Oh, don't get me started on that silly Duncan woman,' he told me. 'Did you know she strangled herself with her own scarf?'

'What do you mean?' I asked.

I listened, wide-eyed, as he recounted the story of how Isadora Duncan was a real lady and used to love wearing these long, floaty scarves.

'She lived in France, and she was coming over a bridge one day and her long scarf got caught in the axle of the convertible car that she was in and it strangled her. Broke her neck right there on the spot.'

My grandmother was a cold, unemotional woman but she was a fantastic seamstress and dressmaker, and I'd sit there for ages and watch her work. One day she was making a beautiful blue gown that had silk ribbons from the waist down with an underskirt underneath, and at the end of every ribbon there was a silver bell. It was the most beautiful dress that I'd ever seen and I was fascinated.

'Who's that dress for, Gaga?' I asked her.

'This one is for a Russian princess,' she said.

It took her hours to sew all the tiny bells on the bottom.

In the front room she had a beautiful old mahogany sewing desk with her Singer sewing machine on the top and dozens of small drawers underneath that were filled with ribbons, beads and different coloured silks. I loved rummaging round in them and touching all of the treasures that were inside.

'Can I help you tidy up your bits and bobs, Gaga?' I asked her.

'As long as you're careful, Rene,' she told me. 'Don't go pricking your fingers on any needles.'

My biggest wish was for her to make me a princess gown all of my very own. On my fourth birthday she made me a beautiful party dress. It was green cotton with a little collar, puff sleeves and a big bow on the back, and it had frills from the waist down. She even made a matching one for my favourite doll Audrey.

My mum was the eldest of seven children,

although two of her brothers had died as toddlers – one had got diphtheria and the other had fallen into the Thames and drowned. It used to cause no end of arguments between my grandparents, as my grandfather could never remember the names of the two that had died and my grandmother used to get really annoyed with him about it.

'Imagine not remembering your own children,' she used to say to me. 'How could he forget his own flesh and blood?'

Mum wasn't close to her surviving sisters Violet and Winnie or her brothers Arthur and Harry, and they didn't treat her very nicely. They were all very snobby and wealthy, and they looked on her as a failure when she came back to live with her parents, even though she was a widow. That side of it was all kept from me when I was small, but I began to realise it more as I got older. They didn't like her choice of husband and the way, in their opinion, she had completely changed her views.

Mum and I stuck together, and we were a close little unit. She had a couple of boyfriends when I was very young, although I don't remember meeting them. It was only when I was much older that she told me about one man she actually got engaged to.

'But then he turned around and said that he'd only marry me if I'd agree to put you in a children's home, so I told him to get knotted,' she said.

It's only as I grew up that I started to appreciate how hard it must have been to be a single parent in those days. As I got older, I came to realise that I was different because other children had fathers and I didn't.

'Why haven't I got a daddy like everyone else?' I asked Mum one day. 'Where is my daddy?'

She got a dusty album out of a drawer and showed me a photograph. It was a sepia picture of a handsome young man with blond hair and big, expressive brown eyes and dark eyebrows.

'That was Daddy,' she said gently. 'Your lovely dark eyes are just like his.'

There was another black-and-white photograph of Dad in a helmet and goggles standing next to a motorbike.

'That's him and his beloved motorbike,' she told me. 'He used to strap his cello on the back and go whizzing round London from theatre to theatre.'

Because I didn't remember anything about Dad it was nice to hear stories about him.

'Your father was a very unusual man,' Mum told me. 'He had strong morals about how children should be treated.'

She described how she had been out one day with him and my brother.

'We were walking down the road and your

father saw another man and his son across the street. The boy was only about five and he must have done something naughty so his father gave him a slap around the legs.

'Well, when your father saw this he was so angry. He crossed over the road and told the man in no uncertain terms to never, ever hit his child again. I think the man was a bit shocked getting reprimanded by a complete stranger, but I was so proud of your dad.'

It was the norm for children to get a good hiding in those days, but Mum said my father was dead against it and he would always intervene if he saw someone hitting or shouting at a child or treating them badly.

'Your father was a very gentle man and a great champion of children,' she said. 'He was a natural with them. You had bad colic when you were a tiny baby and he'd sit there for hours playing music from the ballet *The Dying Swan* on his cello trying to soothe you to sleep.'

'He sounds like a lovely daddy,' I said sadly.

Hearing how wonderful and kind he was made me feel even sadder that he wasn't around, and even though I couldn't really remember him I always felt his loss in my life.

The only father figure I had was my brother Raymond. He'd been very close to my father and I don't think that he ever got over his death. People didn't show their feelings in those days, though, and if I ever asked him about my dad, he would clam up.

'I don't want to talk about it, Rene,' he would tell me.

My brother was very academic and clever, and he always bought me books. While other children my age were being read *Winnie the Pooh* or *The Wind in the Willows*, he brought me home the complete works of Charles Dickens and Thomas Hardy.

'Sit down, Rene,' he said one day. 'I'm going to teach you to play chess.'

My father had taught Raymond to play chess and so he decided he was going to teach me. He was a chess whizz but I was four years old and had no interest whatsoever.

'This is so boring,' I moaned as we sat and stared at the checked board.

'Oh, Rene, you're such a fidget, it's all about skill,' he said.

But I preferred something much faster moving, and even though I adored Raymond it didn't interest me in the slightest.

'Oh, I give up,' he said, exasperated. 'One day, Rene, you'll find something that you love doing.'

Even though I was only four years old I was about to stumble across something that would become my biggest passion for the rest of my life.

2

Bows and Bombs

Through the darkness I saw them. Dancing around with their floaty wings like beautiful butterflies.

'Fairies!' I gasped. 'I can see fairies!'

I felt as if I were in a dream and I had never seen anything like it in my life. I just sat there on the edge of my seat with my mouth gaping open as I watched these mystical creatures flitting around the stage.

'Mummy, I want to be one of those,' I whispered. 'I want to be a fairy.'

I was four years old and my mother had taken me to, see my first ever pantomime – *Cinderella* at the Grand Theatre, Clapham Junction. I had loved the pumpkin coach, but when the gauze curtain came down all lit up with twinkly lights and these fairies danced across the stage I was absolutely mesmerised. This was the first time I had seen anyone dance, and from then on that was it. I was hooked for the rest of my life.

'Please can I do that, Mummy?' I asked afterwards. 'Can I dance like a fairy?'

'Well, you could do ballet lessons if you

30

wanted,' she said.

I didn't forget about it, and Mum kept her promise and I started going to a weekly lesson at a local ballet school in Clapham. It was in a big house, and one room had been converted into a ballet studio with huge mirrors and a barre down one side. Each lesson cost 2s. 6d. (two shillings and sixpence), and it must have been a struggle for Mum to afford it, but I loved every minute of it and I lived for that day of the week. Leotards hadn't been invented in those days and tutus were only worn for formal occasions like shows and exams, so I wore a loose black cotton tunic that my grandmother had made me, and I had a piece of pink chiffon wound around my head and tied in a big bow at the back to keep my hair off my face.

I hung on to the ballet mistress's every word, and I memorised each step and practised until it was perfect.

'I'd like you to be Greek slave girls today,' she told us one afternoon. 'I want you to pretend that you're holding a vase as you promenade.'

It was very sad, melancholy music, and as I paraded around the room pretending to hold a heavy Grecian urn on my shoulder I felt in my heart I really was that unhappy little slave girl. So much so, I even felt tears in my eyes as I danced.

At the end of the class, when Mum came

to collect me, my ballet teacher took her to one side.

'I think Irene has great potential,' I heard her say. 'She really seems to feel the music and her timing is spot on.'

That didn't mean anything to me. All I knew was that dancing was just another way of being a fairy and I loved it. But just a few weeks after starting my lessons I suddenly got very ill. I was burning up, and all this horrible stuff was oozing out of my right ear. I was in absolute agony.

'We'd better take you to see the doctor,' said Mum.

I knew it had to be serious for that to happen. These were the days before the National Health Service, and a visit to the doctor's surgery cost a lot of money.

The doctor examined me as I whimpered in pain.

'She has an abscess of the middle ear,' he told my mother. 'You need to get her to hospital straight away. If it's not treated quickly it can be highly dangerous and spread to the brain.'

By then I felt so ill I could barely walk, and Mum had to carry me to St George's Hospital in Tooting. When we got there she passed me to a doctor.

'Say goodbye to your mother,' he told me.

Suddenly I was absolutely terrified. I'd never been away from Mum and I didn't know where they were taking me or what they were going to do to me.

'No!' I yelled. 'I want to stay with Mummy.'

I kicked and screamed and made such a fuss it took three nurses to cart me off. My little body shook with sobs as they held me down on a table while the doctor poured peroxide in my poorly ear. It burned and stung, and I was petrified.

'We have to be cruel to be kind,' he told me. 'This will hopefully kill the infection.'

There was no such thing as antibiotics then. Afterwards my ear was padded up with a big gauze dressing that had to be changed every week.

I was in such a state when they took me back to Mum, who looked really worried.

'It's all right, Rene,' she said, giving me a cuddle. 'You can come home with me now. It's all over.'

'Oh, thank goodness,' I sighed.

I was exhausted but it was such a relief that they weren't keeping me in. I had to go back every week for months so they could put more peroxide in my ear and I was in constant pain. Eventually it seemed to work and thankfully they managed to save my hearing, although I've still got scar tissue in my ear now.

As soon as I was better, Mum started working again. I was a bit older now, and she needed to try to earn some money to help support us. She would spend hours every day practising her violin, and then go to the theatre and perform in the orchestra at night when I was in bed. While she practised I would be left to my own devices to amuse myself, which wasn't hard thanks to my vivid imagination.

One day I took myself off to Clapham Common and lay on my front with my nose in the long grass. I watched ants and ladybirds crawl around and worms slither in the soil, but I wasn't there to look for wildlife.

'Come out,' I whispered. 'I know you're in there somewhere.'

I was there to find the fairies. I stayed like that for hours with my head buried in the grass, just watching and waiting for my favourite creatures to make an appearance. I believed that they were real and I could see them in my head. I knew that all fairies danced, they lived in flowers and they had very long, floaty wings like butterflies or moths. I used to spend hours lying there on the common waiting for them. I never told anyone, though, as I was frightened that they'd make fun of me.

Even now, at the ripe old age of eighty-four, if anyone asks what my religion is I tell them this: 'I believe in fairies at the bottom of the garden!'

It often gets me a few funny looks. But I find it quite sad today that children don't have vivid imaginations any more; they're told so much.

I always say to my granddaughter Billie, 'How do you know that I'm not a fairy?'

So she checked my back and found two little nobbles.

'That's where your wings will grow, Grandma,' she told me.

Now, whenever I see her she checks my back to see if my wings have sprouted yet!

I suppose in a way I was a very lonely child as I was left on my own to get on with everything. Nobody asked me what I wanted to do or where I wanted to go, or thought up things to entertain me, so I had to make my own fun. In one sense it worked in my favour because I didn't have to ask – Mummy, can I do this? I just went and did it. Although Raymond still lived with us, by now he had got a job as an apprentice for a company in central London that manu-factured Bakelite, so he was out at work all day.

I knew my mother loved me and she was very affectionate, but all she lived for was her music. Looking back, I'd say she was very unsociable and introverted; she didn't have friends and never went out. She would practise all day long and go out to work at the theatre at night. She never did anything but play the violin, and spent so many hours practising that I'd get fed up.

'Mummy, I'm bored,' I told her one afternoon.

'Rene, only boring people get bored,' she said.

So I decided to take myself off on an adventure. I walked down to Clapham and caught the No. 49 bus to the West End. I had a terrific sense of freedom that sadly children don't have these days. Children were very free and I was always either on Clapham Common or Wandsworth Common, playing with friends, or on a Routemaster going somewhere exciting. I paid my tuppence ha'penny (two and a half old pennies) to the conductor and headed into town.

I sat on the top deck and looked out of the window as we went past Battersea Park and down the King's Road. I got off at High Street Kensington and from there headed to Regent Street. I must have walked miles but I knew exactly where I was going – to my favourite place in the whole world, Hamley's toy store. I wandered from floor to floor gazing in awe at the giant teddy bears, the life-size dolls, sailboats and pedal cars. Things I knew that my mother could never afford.

Afterwards I walked down Oxford Street to Selfridges. I loved the sense of grandeur as I saw the doorman in his top hat.

'Good morning, Miss,' he said, and I giggled as he held open the door for me.

In 1938 no one batted an eyelid to see an

eight-year-old wandering round the West End on her own, but if it happened today I'd probably get taken into care by Social Services! There were plenty of other children doing the same thing, and often you'd see gangs of youngsters from the East End going up West to pick pockets.

I loved Selfridges and I knew all the departments like the back of my hand. I'd go straight up to the first floor to look at all the fancy ball gowns. I'd walk along the rails, touching the brightly coloured taffeta dresses and admiring the intricate beading. Sometimes I'd get the lift up to the roof, where I'd watch fashionable ladies and gents going for a promenade around the manicured gardens. There was even a café up there and a women's gun club.

Afterwards I'd saunter along Oxford Street to Hyde Park, where I'd sit by the Serpentine and watch the birds and climb a few trees. Once, I was walking along a secluded path when I noticed a man coming towards me in a mackintosh. Call it a sixth sense, but I could tell straight away that something wasn't right about him. He looked a bit scruffy and his clothes were all grubby. As he got closer he suddenly held his mac open, and I realised that he had his flies undone and his bits and pieces were hanging out for all and sundry to see!

'Eurgh, put it away!' I laughed.

But he just closed his coat, walked past and didn't say a word.

I wasn't scared or frightened, I just thought it was hysterically funny. If that was the way that he got his kicks then good luck to him, I thought. Then I caught the No. 49 home, my stomach rumbling with hunger at the thought of a boiled egg for tea.

In a way, even though I was still only eight I was a pretty savvy and streetwise child. Flashers were very common in those days and most of them seemed harmless to my friends and me. I coped with it better than my poor mother. I remember her coming home one night after work absolutely furious.

'Oh my goodness, Rene,' she said dramatically. 'Something dreadful has just happened. I don't believe it.'

'What is it, Mum?' I asked.

She explained how she had been on the Northern line and she'd been in the carriage on her own when a man had got on.

'I'd just got up as mine was the next stop when he undid his trousers and exposed himself to me.'

'What did you do?' I asked her.

'Well, I marched over to him and said: "How dare you do that to me, you disgusting little man." I was so angry, do you know what I did, Rene?'

'No, Mum.'

I was so cross, I got my violin case and I slammed it down really hard on his you-know-what. Hopefully that will teach him not to do that in a hurry again.'

My mum was a tiny woman, and she looked very prim with her two long plaits that she tied up on the top of her head. I bet he hadn't been expecting her reaction.

'Is your violin all right, Mum?' I asked with a smirk.

Things were still very strained between Mum and her family, and as I got older I became more aware of the tensions. One day I went to visit my Aunty Vi, who lived in Hendon, north London. My mother never came with me, and I liked going because I could play with my cousin Shirley, who was four years older than me.

'Violet's a terrible snob,' my mother warned me as she walked with me to the Tube station. 'Just ignore anything she says to you.'

It wasn't long before Aunty Vi started bragging about my cousin Shirley and how well she was doing at school.

'She's so bright there's no doubt she'll go to university one day,' she said.

'Will I go to university too?' I asked.

Aunty Vi just laughed.

'I doubt that very much, dear,' she said. 'I don't think you're clever enough for university. You'll have probably left long before it's time to do matriculation.'

Matriculation was the exam that you took in high school to determine whether you were clever enough to go on to further education.

'Well, I don't need to go to university,' I told her. 'I'm going to be a ballet dancer.'

'A ballet dancer?' said Aunty Vi, aghast. 'You'll never make a dancer, Rene. You're not pretty enough and I seriously doubt that you've got the talent, either.'

Hearing that sort of criticism at such a young age from someone should have been a crushing blow. But I'd heard it all before, so I just let it wash over me and refused to get angry about it.

It was always the same criticisms that I'd hear time and time again whenever I went over there – I wasn't clever enough, pretty enough, slim enough, rich enough. I got so used to it I didn't even bother answering her back. It didn't matter to me that I was constantly criticised and put down. I didn't really care what my aunties and uncles thought. In a way it made me even more determined.

'I will be a ballet dancer one day,' I told my cousin Shirley. 'Just you wait and see.'

I never told Mum what Aunty Violet had said, though. I knew she would be furious and I didn't want to make the rift between her and her sisters any bigger.

Sometimes it was just as bad at home. I was always very loyal to my mother, and I hated it when my grandparents would criticise her to my face.

One day my grandfather was grumbling about her and saying how she never had enough money. Anyone could say what they liked about me, but when it came to my mother it was a completely different matter. I had a sparky temper and if someone pushed the wrong buttons then I wasn't frightened of speaking my mind.

'Don't you dare run Mummy down like that, Papa,' I told him.

'I don't know why you always stick up for your mother,' he said. 'She's a failure and she should have never married that father of yours.'

'She's doing the best she can,' I shouted.

My grandfather had a typical Victorian attitude to children – he thought they should be seen and not heard – and he was furious that I'd answered him back.

'Don't speak to me like that, young lady,' he bellowed. 'I'm going to lock you in your room and see if that teaches you a lesson.'

But when he tried to grab hold of me I went berserk. I lashed out at him, kicking and screaming.

'I won't have you behave like this, Rene,' he yelled. 'You're a silly little girl who's never going to make anything of your life, just like your mother.'

'Yes, I will,' I yelled. 'I'm going to be a dancer.'

'A dancer?' he scoffed. 'I doubt that very much.'

When Mum got home and I told her what had happened she didn't seem surprised. She knew what her father was like.

'I think it's time that we tried to find somewhere else to live,' she told me. 'We need our own space.'

I knew that she found it a strain living with her parents and a few weeks later we moved out. Mum had found a job as a carer for an old spinster called Miss Higgins, who was paralysed from the chest down after contracting polio as a child and was completely bed-bound. We'd save money on rent because we'd be living with the old lady in her 1920s semi-detached house in Norbury. She had the downstairs, and Raymond, Mum and I had the upstairs. Miss Higgins was obviously wealthy, as the house was nicely decorated and pristine, but it was clear from the start that Mum hated every minute of it.

'Oh, that woman,' she said. 'She just treats me like a dogsbody. It's no wonder that she never has any visitors.'

She'd gone through several carers before Mum, and it wasn't hard to see why. Miss Higgins wasn't very pleasant, and Mum was at her beck and call day and night. She had to give her a bed bath, make her meals, and do her shopping and the cleaning.

Mum had just sat down one night when we heard the familiar tinkle of the bell that Miss Higgins rang when she needed something.

'Give me strength,' Mum sighed through gritted teeth. 'That woman will be the death of me.'

I went down with her.

'Can the child come and sit with me for a while?' she said as she saw me lurking in the doorway.

'I suppose so,' said Mum. 'Rene, come and talk to Miss Higgins.'

'Do I have to?' I sighed, but just one look at Mum's stern face and I didn't dare say another word.

I sat and stared at Miss Higgins. She always looked very straight-laced and she never, ever smiled. She had long white hair, and a white frilly nightie with a high collar and a knitted bed jacket on. Her bed was white, too, and she was half propped up with a pile of pillows. She was a bit like Miss Havisham in *Great Expectations*, a strange ghostly figure all in white. I wasn't frightened of her, I just thought she was the most peculiar woman that I'd ever seen.

She stared at me with a very disapproving look on her face. 'Talk to me child,' she said.

'Do you like arithmetic?'

I shook my head.

'Well, what do you like doing then?'

I shrugged my shoulders.

'What's the matter?' she asked. 'Cat got your tongue?'

'Rene, don't be so rude and answer Miss Higgins,' Mum told me.

'I like w-w-riting stories,' I stammered. 'And d-d-drawing.'

You see, that was the real reason why I didn't want to chat to her. I didn't want this strange old woman to know that I had a terrible stammer as I was really embarrassed about it.

My brother Raymond had developed a very bad stammer after our father had died, and when I turned four I had started stammering too.

'Are you sure you're not just copying your brother?' Mum had asked.

But I knew I wasn't. I just couldn't stop myself stammering. I was fine with my friends and family and people that I knew, but with strangers it was a different story. I would get nervous and I would hesitate and the words just wouldn't come out, or I'd be halfway through a sentence and I couldn't finish it without gasping for breath.

'I can't understand what you're saying to me, dear,' said Miss Higgins.

'She just stammers a bit sometimes, that's

all,' Mum told her. It was so frustrating sometimes. Like the morning that there was a frantic knocking on the front door.

'Run and get that, Rene, will you,' said Mum.

I went downstairs and opened the door to find the coal man standing there. He was in a terrible state.

'Me 'orse,' he said in his broad cockney accent. 'Me bleedin' 'orse is dead. He had an 'art attack comin' up the 'ill.'

I looked out and there was the coal man's huge white horse lying in the middle of the street. Every day the horse would lumber up the hill near us pulling tonnes of coal in his cart, and then the coal man would tip it down the chute outside each house that led to the cellar so we could all light our fires and ranges.

I wanted to say how sorry I was about his horse, but no matter how hard I tried the words just wouldn't come out.

'I-I-I-,' I stammered. 'S-s-s-.'

'I don't understand you, love,' he said, 'Is yer old man in? I need some 'elp to try and drag him out of the street.'

It was so frustrating. All I could do was run upstairs to get Mum, sobbing at the thought of the coal man's beautiful horse lying dead in our road.

There was no help for people with stammers in those days. It wasn't something that you went to see the doctor about, and there was no such thing as a speech therapist. It was just seen as something you had to live with and hopefully grow out of, which was what Raymond had done as he'd got older.

One weekend Mum took me to the hairdressers as a treat. I had dead straight hair, and since I was little I'd always worn it in long plaits like my mother with two ribbons on the end.

'Please can I have my hair cut?' I'd begged her for months.

So we went to the local hairdressers and they chopped it into a bob and pinned a big orange bow on the top.

The next day Mum and I were walking back from the shops to our house and I was proudly showing off my new haircut. I was still wearing the bow that the hairdresser had pinned in it.

I was skipping along, hand in hand with Mum, when suddenly we heard a strange noise above us. I stared up into the sky to see what was making the racket.

'Look, Mummy!' I shouted.

There were two planes looping and rolling all over the place, and they were flying so low I could hear the machine-gun fire and see the sparks as the bullets bounced off their wings.

'Wow!' I gasped.

I thought it was really exciting to have this

battle going on right above our heads, but Mum looked terrified. Much to my surprise, she pushed me into a hedge.

'Get down, Rene,' she said. 'Don't move.'

'But my bow!' I said. 'I don't want to squash my brand new bow.'

'Don't worry about your blessed bow – just stay there and don't move,' she hissed.

I could see the fear in her eyes as she crouched down in the dirt with me.

'What is it, Mum?' I asked. 'Why are those two planes shooting at each other?'

'It's the war,' she said. 'I think it's started.'

It was Sunday, 3 September 1939 and life as we knew it was about to change beyond all recognition because of a man called Adolf Hitler.

3

Painful Goodbyes

I watched out of the window as my mother dragged the old settee into the garden. Then she got a saw and started sawing the arms and the back off it. It was hard work but she was strong and determined, and even though it took her the best part of an hour she managed it in the end.

'Rene, come and help me pull it into the shelter so we've got something to sleep on tonight,' she yelled.

As part of the Government issue, an Anderson shelter had been built at the bottom of our garden. It was a little brick hut sunk into the ground, with a corrugated-iron roof and a door at one end.

Now the war had started, the air-raid siren would sound every evening and we'd go in there as it got dark to save us from having to get up in the middle of the night and run outside in the pitch black. It was just Mum and me, as Miss Higgins refused to leave the house.

'I'm going nowhere,' she told us defiantly. 'I've not been out of bed for fifty-odd years, and I'm certainly not going to start now just because of the Jerries and some silly war. If the house gets bombed and goes down, then I'm going down with it.'

I think Mum was relieved that she didn't have to carry her out there every night, and it was fine by me as the shelter wasn't very big and I didn't fancy being squashed up with that strange old lady. It was dark and dank, so Mum was determined to make it as cosy as possible for us. I helped her drag the settee in there, and that night it made a comfy bed for us to lie on. Mum had got a little oil heater and a paraffin lamp, and we snuggled down under a big eiderdown.

'You see,' she said. 'It's nice and snug in here now.'

We had all sorts of woollies on, too, to keep warm – jumpers, socks and even a scarf, and a hot-water bottle each.

'It's lovely, Mummy,' I told her. 'It's like we're on an adventure.'

The war was all a big game to me but I could tell that Mum was scared. She was very nervous and on edge, I could sense it.

By the time the air-raid siren went off we'd already been in the shelter for hours.

'Here we go again,' she said, cuddling up to me.

I soon learned to recognise the different sounds of war, and lying there listening I'd hear the familiar drone of German bombers dropping their loads on London as they followed the path of the Thames. The bombs made their own distinctive noise when they fell – a sort of whistling, whooshing sound, and then there would be an ominous second of silence before impact.

Tonight the planes sounded very close and Mum jumped every time a bomb came down. The ground shook and we heard fragments of metal hitting the roofs of nearby houses as the bombs exploded.

'Shall I have a little peep outside to see what's going on?' I asked.

But Mum looked horrified.

'No, you will not, Rene,' she told me.

'You're staying safely in here.'

I was disappointed, as I'd imagined the sky glowing orange and red from all the fires.

'I hope Raymond's all right,' said Mum.

Instead of coming home, he often spent the night sleeping in one of the Tube stations so he could get up and go straight to work the next day. Hundreds of others did this too, and by 6 p.m. people started setting up for the night, reserving their spot. You'd see them clutching blankets and pillows, and women sat there on the platforms in curlers, putting cold cream on their faces.

It didn't take long before I was out like a light, lulled to sleep by the sound of the gunfire and the bombs falling all around us. When we woke up in the morning it was freezing as we crawled out of the shelter and back into the house. Mum had to get breakfast for Miss Higgins, and I had to get ready to go to school.

Our area of south London had been quite badly bombed and as I walked to school I saw that one of the houses in a nearby street had been hit. There were soldiers helping to clear up the debris, and the people who lived there were sorting through the rubble, desperately trying to salvage some of their possessions.

During the war years this became a normal sight. The roads were littered with bits of barrage balloon and shrapnel – pieces of bombs and bullets. I stopped to pick up a few nice silvery bits that I knew would get some admiring glances from the other children at school.

Every child was issued with a gas mask that we had to carry around at all times. Well-to-do children kept theirs in leather or plastic boxes, but mine was in a cardboard box with a string handle so I could carry it over my shoulder. It was all a big game to us. Sometimes the air raids would be during the daytime so we'd have practice runs at school. One morning the siren went off and we all trooped down to the cellar. We sat there having an arithmetic lesson with our gas masks on. They were made of rubber, and had goggles and something that was a bit like a coffee filter at the end of the nose – I found them ever so claustrophobic. So to stop me from feeling frightened and take my mind off wearing one, I decided to make it into a bit of a joke.

'Look, you can make rude noises,' I said, blowing a raspberry into my mask.

Everyone laughed and thought it was hilarious, and soon every pupil in my class was doing the same thing. Unfortunately the teachers weren't amused as we didn't get much work done.

I can't ever remember anyone being upset or frightened during the air raids at school. It became part of our daily lives and we just accepted that that's what happened.

A lot of children were evacuated to the countryside, but Mum refused point blank to let me go.

'You're staying here with me,' she said.

I was so grateful for that. She was all I had in the world, and while the bombs didn't scare me, being away from her would have terrified me.

Thankfully none of our family were injured or killed, although Mum's brother, my Uncle Harry, had a bit of a close shave. We received a letter from him one morning telling us how an incendiary bomb had landed on his doorstep, and he hadn't realised and opened the door.

'Poor Uncle Harry,' she said. 'The bomb went off straight in his face.'

'Is he all right, Mum?' I asked.

'Oh yes,' she said. 'It gave him a bit of a fright and singed all his eyebrows off, but apart from that he's fine.'

Even though it was mean, we couldn't help but have a bit of a chuckle about it.

The war also brought me a new playmate. I became best friends with a pretty little blonde girl called Diana Baracnik, whose family moved into our street after fleeing from Czechoslovakia. We'd climb trees or go to dance classes together, and after school I'd go round to her house and play dollies. I loved my dolls and I had about six of them.

Some of them were china and some were papier mâché.

One person who felt very strongly about the war was my brother Raymond. He'd always been a socialist like my father and he shared his strong views.

'Wars and violence don't solve anything, Rene,' he told me. 'Nobody wins in war.'

He didn't want any part of it and he was one of those known as conscientious objectors – people who for social or religious reasons refused to go to war.

During the First World War conscientious objectors were seen as criminals and sent to prison. Women would wander round and hand any man who was the right age and not wearing a military uniform a white chicken feather, which was a symbol of cowardice, to shame them into enlisting. Several conscientious objectors killed themselves because they couldn't cope with the stigma. During the Second World War the punishment wasn't as severe, but you could still be arrested for refusing to do National Service and you had to appear in front of a tribunal to explain your reasons why. Despite the risks, Mum respected Raymond's opinion as she shared similar beliefs.

'Your father would have been so proud of Raymond,' she told me. 'I know he would have done exactly the same if he was here now.'

Mum had told me many times that my father was strongly anti-war. Because of his bad asthma he wasn't called up during the First World War, but his older brother Raymond had been.

'Raymond was a tail gunner, and the first time he went up he was shot and killed instantly,' said Mum. 'Your father was heart-broken. He said his poor brother was just cannon fodder and that only reinforced his anti-war stance.'

It seemed apt that my brother had been named after our late Uncle Raymond.

One morning we were all having our breakfast when there was a loud rap on the front door.

'Open up,' shouted a gruff voice. 'It's the police.'

Mum looked at Raymond in a panic. I didn't have a clue what was going on.

'What shall I do?' she whispered to him.

'You'd better go and let them in,' he said. 'I've got nothing to hide.'

Mum went and opened the door, and two officers came marching up the stairs and into our dining room.

'Raymond Bott?' one of them said to my brother.

'Yes,' he replied.

'Young man, I'm afraid we're going to have to arrest you for failing to register for National Service,' he said, pulling him up from his chair. 'Come with us, please.'

'I'm a conscientious objector,' he told them. 'I don't believe in war.'

'Well, you will have to appear in front of a tribunal and tell them your reasons for that. Then they will decide what will happen to you,' the other one said.

Mum burst into tears.

'You can't do this,' she sobbed. 'You can't just take him away like this.'

'I'm afraid we have to,' one of them said, leading him off down the stairs. 'We're just obeying orders.'

My brother didn't say a word, and he wasn't allowed to take anything with him. My mother was inconsolable, and I could hear Miss Higgins frantically ringing her bell downstairs, probably trying to find out what all the fuss was about.

I just sat there eating my toast, completely stunned by this drama that was happening over breakfast.

Mum followed the officers downstairs, and I ran to the window and watched as they pushed Raymond into the back of the police car and drove away. A few neighbours had come out of their houses to see what was going on too, and they all stood there staring. Mum came upstairs sobbing.

'I can't believe this has happened,' she cried.

The following evening after school I called

at my friend Diana's house as usual. Her father answered the door.

'I'm sorry, Irene,' he said. 'You won't be able to play with Diana any more or come round to our house.'

'But why!' I asked. 'She's my best friend.'

'You'd better ask your mother,' he told me.

I went home in floods of tears to Mum.

'Diana's dad says I'm not allowed to be her friend any more,' I sobbed. 'I don't understand.'

'He probably heard about what happened to Raymond,' she said. 'A lot of people don't agree with your brother's views about the war.'

'But what do you mean?' I asked. 'What's that got to do with Diana's dad?'

'He probably thinks that Raymond's a coward for not wanting to fight the Nazis,' she explained. 'Perhaps his family had a bad time in their country, which is why they came over here.'

I was devastated that I'd lost my best friend. I couldn't understand what difference the war and my brother's beliefs made to whom I could and couldn't play with.

But it wasn't just a one-off. Word soon spread among our neighbours that Raymond had been taken off by the police, and after that a lot of people wouldn't talk to Mum or me. They'd see us in the street, put their head down and walk straight past us. There was a huge stigma attached to being a conscientious objector, or a 'conchie' as they were nicknamed. A lot of people associated it with being a coward, but in fact most conscientious objectors were motivated by religious reasons.

Raymond had to appear in front of a tribunal that would decide whether to give him an exemption, dismiss his application and send him to fight, or make him do non-combatant work. A week later we received a letter from him.

The tribunal decided that I should be sent to work in the Pioneer Corps where they have given me the task of digging up roads. It's hard labour and the days are long but at least I have stuck to my principles and I'm not involved in any way with the taking of lives. I'm stationed at a barracks in Lincolnshire and ironically most of my fellow conscientious objectors are extremely religious so they are slightly bemused at being billeted with an atheist like me who is constantly questioning their beliefs.

Mum was relieved that he was all right, although she was annoyed by the type of work Raymond was doing.

'What a waste of his talents,' she sighed. 'He's far too clever to be digging up roads.'

His superiors must have realised that too, as soon Raymond wrote to us again to say that he had been transferred to the Army Service Corps, where he was given the job of drawing maps. Part of his role eventually involved helping to plan the D-Day landings, which he justified by saying it was about saving lives rather than taking them.

Despite the war, daily life at home went on as normally as possible. By the time I was ten, however, Mum had run out of patience with Miss Higgins.

'I can't look after that woman for a second longer or I swear I will kill her,' she told me.

But work in the orchestras was in short supply during the war as some theatres had been badly bombed and were forced to close. Things were going to be tight financially again, so we were forced to move back in with my grandparents.

The day before we left the house in Norbury, a government inspector came out to check all the Anderson shelters in the street. Mum and I watched as he tapped the mortar between the bricks. To our horror, it crumbled instantly and his finger went straight through it.

'Shoddy workmanship,' he sighed, shaking his head. 'If a bomb had dropped on that thing it would have been curtains for you two.'

Mum and I stared at each other in shock.

'I don't believe it,' she said. 'To think we've been sleeping in there every night for nearly two years thinking that we were safe.'

By this time my grandparents had rented out their attic room to a ninety-year-old spinster called Miss Smythe, so Mum and I had to live on the much bigger and lighter second floor of the house. It felt like a palace compared with the poky, cramped attic. We had two bedrooms, and our own living-room and bathroom. Moving back to Battersea meant that I had to change schools to Honeywell Road Primary, but I still did my ballet lessons, which I absolutely loved.

One day Mum sat me down.

'What do you want to do when you grow up, Rene?' she asked.

I knew my answer straight away, because since I was a little girl I'd only ever wanted to do one thing.

'I want to be a ballet dancer,' I said. 'I want to be on the stage.'

A lot of other parents at that time might have just laughed or told me I would have to go out and get a proper job, be a teacher or a secretary, but Mum didn't flinch.

'All right, then,' she said. 'You'll have to go to stage school if you're really serious about doing that. Where would you like to go?'

'Italia Conti,' I said without hesitation.

It was the world's oldest and most prestigious theatre arts training school, the one that the older girls at dance class always talked about. I didn't ever think in a million years that Mum would be able to afford to send me to stage school, but to my surprise she didn't question it.

'Very well,' she said. 'I'll contact Italia Conti and get some more information.'

Mum kept her promise and a few days later she told me what they had said.

'It's £20 a term,' she told me.

My heart sank. That was a heck of a lot of money in those days, and I knew it was the end of my big dream. As a single mother who went from one job to the next as a violinist, there was no way she could afford expensive stage-school fees like that.

But in 1942 Mum made the biggest sacrifice of her life for me. She sat me down one day and took hold of my hands.

'There's something I need to tell you, Rene,' she said. 'I think I've found a solution to our problems. I've decided to join ENSA.'

ENSA stood for the Entertainments National Service Association, a group of performers who travelled around the world during the Second World War to entertain British troops and keep up morale. They had everything from singers, dancers and musicians to comedians, bird impersonators, contortionists and even roller skaters.

'The pay is good, and having a regular wage is the only way that I can afford to put you through stage school,' she said. 'It means that I'll be away from home for a while, but you can stay here with Papa and Gaga. They're going to post me to Egypt, where I'll perform as part of a quartet.'

It was a huge shock, and I couldn't believe she was prepared to do that to help me achieve my dream.

Things moved so quickly. A week later I sat on my mother's bed watching her put on her new ENSA uniform, which consisted of a khaki shirt and belted jacket, an A-line skirt with a pleat up the middle, and a peaked hat. It hadn't really sunk in yet that she was going thousands of miles away and I wouldn't see her for years.

'Come on, then,' she said, holding out one hand to me while in the other one she clutched her beloved violin. 'It's time to go.'

We caught the Tube to the Coliseum, the theatre from where the new recruits were departing. As we walked towards the entrance I could see a big fleet of three-tiered coaches waiting outside. It was pandemonium as hundreds of performers in ENSA uniforms said tearful goodbyes to their families. Mum handed someone her violin to load into the bottom section that was filled with an array of musical instruments. Then she turned to me and gave me a cuddle and a kiss.

'Oh, Rene, I really don't want to leave you,' she said, tears welling up in her eyes.

'Oh, don't worry, I'll be all right,' I said, as

I hated to see her upset.

'I love you very much,' she told me.

Then she turned and walked away. I could see her dabbing her eyes with her hankie as she climbed onto the coach. I watched her take her jacket off, and as she sat down and waved to me through the window that's when it finally hit me.

This was really happening. She was really going.

The only person in the world besides my brother that I loved with all my heart was leaving me.

I was in such a state of shock I couldn't even cry.

As I watched her coach drive away I felt completely and utterly alone in the world.

I got the Tube home in a daze. I was used to being on my own and I was fiercely independent, but it felt very frightening at the age of twelve not having anyone looking out for me. With Mum and Raymond both away, there was literally nobody in my life that I could go to. No-one to give me a kiss or a cuddle, or who would make sure that I was all right and put me first in the world. My grandparents weren't interested, that was for sure.

When I got in that evening they didn't ask me anything about Mum or whether she had got off OK or if I was all right. But as I walked through the door I couldn't hold back my emotion any longer and I burst into tears.

'Whatever's the matter?' my grandmother asked.

'I'm just really sad about Mum going away,' I sobbed.

'Oh, don't be so selfish,' she said.

I knew that was the way it was going to be and I just had to get used to it. Nobody was going to say what I so desperately wanted to hear right now, things like 'Oh, come here and give me a cuddle, Rene, I know you're missing Mummy. Sit down and let's write to her together.'

Nope, I was by myself now. Raymond was still in his barracks up north and Mum was on her way to Africa.

That night it was hard going to sleep on my own. For all of my life I'd had Mum there beside me, but I knew I had to pull myself together and get on with it.

She had done this for me because she wanted me to achieve my dream of going to performing arts school. I had an interview with Italia Conti coming up, and I knew that I had to pass it. I had to get in. For Mum's sake and for mine.

4

Fairyland

Walking towards the heavy black door, I swallowed the lump in my throat. Today was the day that I'd been waiting for. It was my audition at Italia Conti, the country's most prestigious theatre arts school.

As usual I was here on my own. My grand-parents hadn't said a word when I'd told them about the audition. No 'Good luck, dear' or 'I hope it goes well.' Not that I'd expected them to say anything or take any interest in what I was doing, as I knew by now that wasn't going to happen. I knew that it was down to me to do this. Mum had sacrificed everything and gone away so that I could achieve my dream, and I had to get in.

My tummy was churning with a strange mixture of nerves and excitement as I walked up to the front door of Tavistock Little Theatre in Tavistock Square where the school was based. It was an old Victorian building and nothing fancy, but as soon as I pushed open that black door I entered a hive of activity.

Like a Tardis, it opened up inside to reveal

several huge rehearsal rooms. There were girls running past in their black dance tunic uniforms, and every time a door opened I could hear the faint tinkle of a piano, the clatter of tap shoes or someone singing scales. I instantly felt at home and I knew this was where I wanted to be, singing and dancing all day long.

I stopped one of the girls going past.

'Hello, I'm here for an audition,' I told her, thankful that I hadn't stammered.

'I'll go and get Miss Conti for you,' she said.

A few minutes later one of the doors opened and a middle-aged lady with short, dark hair came out.

'Hello, I'm Rene... I mean Irene Bott,' I said. 'I'm here for an audition.'

'Wonderful to meet you, Irene,' she said. 'I'm Ruth Conti, Italia's niece.'

Before she left, Mum had told me that Italia Conti, or old Mrs Conti as everyone called her, was still around but she was in her seventies now and so her niece Ruth had come over from Australia to help run the school.

'You'll have to excuse us,' she said. 'Our old school in Lamb Conduit Street was bombed out by the Germans last year, so the theatre have kindly lent us their rehearsal rooms until we can find some new premises.'

'Oh,' I said. 'I hope no one was hurt.'

She shook her head.

'Thankfully all of the staff and pupils were on tour at the time with one of our shows. It was our poor building that took the brunt of the Nazis but we're managing to muddle through.

'I see you've brought your dance bag,' she said. 'Get yourself changed and then you can join in a ballet class first.'

'Thank you, Miss Conti,' I said.

Even though she seemed friendly, I could tell by the steely look in her eyes that she wouldn't take any nonsense. As I got dressed into my dance tunic I started to feel very nervous and overwhelmed.

You can do this, Rene, I told myself.

I followed Miss Conti into an old, draughty rehearsal room, where lots of girls and a few boys were waiting. There was a ballet barre running down one side and big mirrors. The windows were all blacked out because of the war, so the room was lit by dim electric light. Miss Conti led me over to the front of the room where two women were talking. One was very tall and masculine looking. She had bobbed straight hair and was wearing trousers, and I couldn't help but notice the big stick in her hand.

'Hello, dear,' she said. 'Come in and join us. Have you done much ballet before?'

'I've been going to classes since I was four,' I said.

The other teacher couldn't have been more different. She was small and feminine and had her hair pulled up in a bun, a floaty skirt on and a face full of make-up.

'I'm Toni Shanley,' said the tall, fearsome lady. 'And this is my sister Moira Shanley.

'Take your place and let's begin. Just do what you can.'

'Yes, Miss Toni,' I said.

A grey-haired lady in a flowery dress was sitting at a piano in the corner with a cigarette hanging out of her mouth. Miss Toni gave her a nod and she starting playing, puffing away on her cigarette with a bored look on her face.

'Ready, girls,' said Miss Toni. 'Heads up, straight backs.'

As we stretched, she walked down the length of the barre correcting people by giving them a sharp rap with her stick.

'Bottoms in, shoulders down,' she yelled, coming down the row towards me.

'Chin up, chest up,' she said, lifting up my head with her finger and pressing in my rib cage. 'Carry on, dear.'

I was nervous, as I knew both Miss Shanleys were watching me closely, but I was also very determined. I managed to follow every step and carry on until the end, but I didn't have a clue how it had gone.

'Well done, Irene,' said Miss Moira after class. 'You're a good little dancer. I think

Miss Ruth wants you to go to drama and elocution now.'

She seemed very sweet and gentle compared with her fearsome sister.

I hoped it had gone well but I was terrified that I wasn't good enough. I knew I could do ballet, but I'd only been to my little local class and I'd only briefly had a few tap lessons.

If Miss Toni was scary, the drama teacher was the most terrifying woman that I'd ever seen in my life. She was wearing a long fur coat that dragged on the ground behind her and a huge Russian fur hat.

'Don't mind Miss Margaret,' one of the boys whispered to me. 'She's a bit of a dragon.'

'I can see that,' I said

She was very theatrical and what people might call a bit of a 'luvvie'.

'Come in, de-arr,' she said in a big, booming voice when she saw me lurking by the door. 'I'd like you to recite some Shakespeare for the class today.'

My heart started to pound with nerves.

'Up on the stage?' I said. 'In front of everyone?'

'Yes, de-arr,' she said. 'Is that a problem?'

'N-no,' I said.

I didn't normally get nervous but suddenly I was the most frightened that I'd ever been in my life. It wasn't the fact that I'd never done drama before that was bothering me; it was my stutter that I was worried about. Would they give me a place at stage school if they knew that I stammered?

My legs felt like jelly as I stood on the stage and Miss Margaret passed me the play. It was one of Macbeth's well-known speeches.

The whole room was deadly silent and all eyes were on me. My hands were shaking as I scanned the words.

Is this a dagger which I see before me?
The handle toward my hand? Come, let me clutch thee.

You can do this, Rene, I told myself.

I took a deep breath.

'I-is th-this a d-d-d-...'

B's and d's were particularly tricky for me to say, and no matter how hard I tried, the words just wouldn't come out. I completely panicked and started gasping for breath.

I seemed to be up there for ever, but finally Miss Margaret waved her hand to stop me.

'I see you have a stammer, dear,' she boomed.

'Y-yes,' I said, ashamed and completely mortified that I'd shown myself up in front of the whole class

'Let's leave it there, then,' she said.

I felt sick afterwards. She didn't say anything else, but I was so worried that I had blown my chances.

Next up was a tap class, where the teacher was a tiny woman with jet-black hair and bright red lipstick. I much preferred ballet to tap, but I'd done a little bit before and managed to follow all the steps.

At the end of the morning, Miss Conti called me in to see her.

'Well, Irene, I've had a chat to the teachers,' she said.

I could feel my heart thumping out of my chest. I didn't know what I'd do if they didn't want me. How would I tell Mum that I'd failed?

'By all reports you're a lovely little dancer,' she said. 'A few other areas need a bit of work but we'll take you.'

'Pardon?' I gasped. 'Really?'

'Yes, dear,' she smiled. 'I'll give you a list of what you'll need to bring with you to class. You can start next week.'

I couldn't believe it, I was on cloud nine. I'm going to be a dancer, I thought, triumphantly. I'd done it! I couldn't wait to write to Mum and tell her the news when I had an address for her. It really was a dream come true. I was going to spend every day doing what I loved and was so passionate about.

'Gaga, Papa, I got into Italia Conti!' I told them excitedly when I got home.

'Very good, Rene,' said my grandmother, not even bothering to look up from her needlework. I didn't expect to get glowing accolades, but it would have been nice for them to acknowledge it. After all, they always seemed so proud of their other grandchildren who were all very academic and had gone off to good schools and universities.

The only downside of starting at Italia Conti was that I would have to leave Honeywell Road Primary, where I was very happy. I had a wonderful teacher there called Mrs Ritchie, and I couldn't wait to tell her my news.

'Mrs Ritchie, I got into Italia Conti,' I told her with a big grin. 'I start next week.'

'Well, that is excellent news,' she said.

At the end of the day, she called me over to her and pulled out a chair from under the table.

'Stand up there, Rene,' she said in a loud voice. 'Now tell the rest of the class what you're going to be.'

'I'm going to stage school and I'm going to be a ballet dancer,' I said proudly.

The whole class clapped and gave me three cheers. She was the only person to recognise my achievement and it felt lovely to have someone making a fuss of me. It made me feel really special and I've never forgotten that.

Even though I was sad to leave school I couldn't wait to start at Italia Conti. I spent the next week getting all of the things that I needed for class. Thankfully Mum had left me some money for any extras that I might need. My grandmother made my uniform, which was a black sleeveless satin tunic with two slits up the side and tied in a bow at the back, and black cotton gym knickers.

One afternoon I got the bus up to Covent Garden and went to Frederick Freed's in St Martin's Lane, which I'd heard was *the* place for professional dancers to get their shoes.

'I'd like some dance shoes, please,' I told the shop assistant. 'I need some bright red tap shoes with bows, pink ballet shoes and pink satin pointe shoes.'

'Well, that's quite a list, Miss,' she said. 'Are you here with your mother?'

'No,' I said. 'I'm here on my own.'

Thankfully she knew what she was doing and fitted them for me. There's something special about dance shoes when they're brand new, and I loved every minute of it. The shop assistants made such a fuss of me and brought out about a dozen pairs of ballet shoes all in different shades of pink satin. I loved the pointe shoes the most, as I'd never done pointe work before and that was what prima ballerinas wore. They were stuffed with papier mâché in the toes.

'They're beautiful,' I sighed. 'I can't wait to learn to dance on those.'

'You'll have to get your mother to sew the ribbons on,' the shop assistant told me.

72

'Oh, my mother's not around at the minute,' I told her. 'I can do it myself.'

It was special pink ribbon that was satin on one side and cotton on the other, so they didn't slip when you tied them around your ankles.

'It's important to get them just right,' the woman at Freed's told me. 'Not too tight, not too loose.

'You also need to darn the ends with embroidery cotton so they don't wear out and place a lamb's wool pad on your toes to protect them.'

I also had to sew the elastic straps on my flat satin ballet pumps.

I went home with my head spinning about all the things I had to remember to do. Although I'd been taught needlework at school, I wasn't much good at it, but I was determined to do it and not have to ask my grandmother for help. So I spent the next few evenings sewing away for hours. God knows what sort of a job I did, but I was so proud that I'd done it all myself.

Soon it was time for my first day and I was filled with excitement as well as a few nerves. Walking through those doors at Italia Conti felt to me like going into fairyland. I wasn't even disheartened when the first person I saw was Miss Margaret, the drama teacher.

'Hello,' I said nervously. 'I'm here for my first day.'

'What's your name, de-arr, and I'll put you down on the register?' she asked.

'Irene,' I said. 'Irene Bott.'

Miss Margaret put down her fountain pen and gave me a look of utter disdain.

'Excuse me?' she said.

'Irene Bott,' I repeated.

She fixed her steely gaze on me.

'Bott?' she boomed. 'You can't possibly come to Italia Conti with a name like Bott. Come back tomorrow with a new name.'

'Oh – er, all right then,' I said.

I'd never thought there was anything particularly wrong with my name. She never said why, but perhaps she thought that Bott was too much like bottom. I wouldn't have dreamed of saying no to her, but I worried about it all day.

By the time I got home that evening I'd really started to panic. How was I going to come up with this new name? Pluck one out of thin air completely at random?

I went up to my bedroom and was flicking through my favourite comics for inspiration when I noticed the name of one of the characters in the *Beano* – Sylvia Starr, ace reporter.

'That's it!' I said.

The next day I went back and Miss Margaret was waiting there with the register.

'So have you got a new name, de-aar?'

'Yes,' I said proudly. 'I want to be called

Irene Starr.'

She looked at me in disgust and said, 'Well, I suppose that will have to do then, won't it?'

From then on, Irene Bott didn't exist any more. I was always known as Irene Starr.

A few days later a letter arrived from Mum. I had written to her to tell her all my news but it took weeks for the mail to get through to the troops. It was lovely to see the familiar scrawl of her handwriting.

Dearest Rene,

I was so pleased to hear that you won a place at Italia Conti and I bet you are enjoying doing your beloved dancing all day. Don't worry about the fees, I have contacted Miss Conti directly and taken care of them from here.

It was clear from her letter that my mother was enjoying travelling and she was really taken with Egypt.

It's so different to performing in the orchestra of the big London theatres. Our 'stage' is four wooden planks of wood resting across oil drums or ammunition boxes. There are a couple of shoddy dancers, a singer (if you can call her that) and I'm one of a quartet of musicians. Some people have cruelly nicknamed ENSA 'Every Night Something Awful' but we are doing the best we can to entertain the troops and keep up their morale in difficult circumstances. Despite all the hardships, I am finding it fascinating experiencing another culture so different to ours.

Mum still had her strong principles, though, and she described how one day she had seen a little boy begging in one of the villages. She had gone over and given him some money but the sheikh of the village had seen her.

This man with a long beard wearing a robe came and snatched the money off the poor boy and put it into his own pocket. Well, Rene, you know me. I went berserk. I ran over to him and said: 'Don't you dare do that. Give it back.' I think the fellow was stunned that a woman, and one as tiny as me, would challenge him. I know I could probably have got into all sorts of bother but he did as I asked.

I smiled at the thought of the man's shocked face as my mother had come marching over to him and given him what for. I bet he hadn't been expecting that!

Love you and miss you, Rene.
  Love always,
  Mum xx

She'd sent me a black-and-white photo of her sitting by the Suez Canal. She looked happy, and I noticed that she'd had her hair cut into a shoulder-length bob, which was probably cooler in the oppressive heat of the desert.

'Oh, Mummy, I miss you,' I sighed, my eyes filling up with tears.

I felt so lonely sometimes but I knew there was no point in moping. I tried to take all the positives from it – like my freedom, for a start. Unlike most twelve-year-olds I never had to ask permission to do anything.

I also loved every minute of being at Italia Conti, and that eased the pain of being parted from Mum. As soon as I walked in the door and heard the tick of a metronome or the tinkle of a piano I felt secure somehow. It was my sanctuary, my escape from the outside world. The war was raging, my family was thousands of miles away from me, but in there I felt safe and I could spend all day doing what I loved, which was dancing.

Everyone there shared the same love of performing and I soon made close friends. I had been worried that, with the fees so high, the other pupils would be from wealthy families, but there were children from more ordinary homes like mine. One of them was a boy named Anthony Newley, who we all called Tony. I liked him straight away because he was fun and loud, and he was always happy and laughing. He was the son of a single mother and he had four siblings.

'I'm an East End lad, Irene,' he told me in his strong cockney accent. 'I'm only 'ere 'cos they gave me a job as an office boy in return for my fees. I ain't no rich, pampered prince.'

He was always joking around and getting ticked off in class. Like the time in tap he pulled funny faces behind the teacher's back as she demonstrated a routine. We all sniggered, but mainly because he hadn't realised that Miss Gertrude had spotted him in the mirror.

'Mr Newley,' she said. 'You're as mad as a March hare. Now please stop larking about.'

'Yes, Miss,' he said, giving me a wink.

He was quite a character, but he was also very talented and you could tell there was something special about him. He had what we would describe today as the X-factor, and I knew he was going to have a bright future in show business.

Another member of our gang was a girl called Nanette Newman. She was a few years younger than me, and she was pretty but very quiet and shy. One of my best friends at Conti's was a stunningly beautiful girl called Daphne Grant. She had bright blue eyes, was very glamorous like Rita Heyworth and had a lovely singing voice. She was an only child and her parents, who were quite elderly, spoiled her rotten. They doted on her and had done absolutely everything for her as she'd grown up. Anything that she asked for, she got, whether it was clothes or jewellery or having a shampoo and set every week at the hairdressers.

No one at Italia Conti dared misbehave. We all knew how lucky we were to be there and we knew the rules – don't be late for class, always be correctly dressed, at the end of a ballet class curtsey to the teacher and the pianist, but clap them after a tap or jazz class.

'You're all here because you want to be,' Miss Conti told us sternly. 'And while you're here I expect you to listen and to work hard. If you don't want to do that, then you're free to go whenever you want.'

I loved the discipline and the structure. The curriculum was a mixture of ballet, tap, contemporary dance, singing, drama and acrobatics. I liked everything except acrobatics, where I struggled to do the forward and backward stopovers, which were like somersaults that you did from a standing position.

Much to my surprise, during my first week at Italia Conti I discovered that I had a good singing voice. Miss Polly, the singing teacher, was an absolute darling. She was potty about Ivor Novello, and she would sit at the piano and go off into some sort of a trance as she played his songs.

'That's wonderful, dear,' she said after I'd sung for her for the first time. 'Absolutely marvellous. You make a lovely mezzo soprano.'

'Do I?' I said.

Singing also had one other bonus.

'My stammer's gone,' I said proudly.

'Of course it has,' she said. 'Have you ever heard a stammering singer?'

I didn't stutter at all when I sang, and after two weeks at Italia Conti my stutter had practically disappeared.

Even though I loved it, they were long days and we worked hard. I'd leave the house at 7 a.m. and it would be after 7 p.m. when I'd get the Tube home. A few weeks after I started there I was allowed to move on to pointe work, which I'd never done before. We were told to rub our feet with surgical spirit every night and then put cold cream on them to try to soften the skin, but I still got blisters from my toes pressing on the pointes. When they split and bled I was in absolute agony.

'What's wrong, Irene?' said Toni Shanley, seeing me wince in class one day.

'My feet are bleeding,' I told her.

I could see the blood seeping through the pink satin on my shoes.

'So?' she said. 'Carry on and put a plaster on them later. You and your feet need to toughen up.'

I knew there was no option but to carry on dancing. You wouldn't dare put a foot wrong in Miss Toni's class, and if you did you'd get a sharp rap from her dreaded stick.

One afternoon we were doing a ballet class with her when suddenly there was an almighty explosion. The walls literally shook, and it felt like the whole building had been lifted up into the air and put back down again.

We all looked at each other, our eyes wide with terror.

'What the heck was that?' Daphne whispered to me.

I didn't know, but I was worried that the whole theatre was about to fall down and collapse on top of us. Miss Toni didn't even flinch, however, and just carried on as if nothing had happened.

'Demi-pliés,' she said. 'Bottoms in, long necks, strong legs.'

I think we were all in a daze, but in a way we were more frightened of Miss Toni and her stick than a German bomb, so we just carried on dancing.

It was only after class that we all gathered round in a huddle.

'Did you hear that?' I said, 'What the heck was it?'

'I think the Jerries just dropped a big one on us,' said Tony Newley.

We all ran to the front door, and as we opened it and walked down the steps I felt glass crunching beneath my feet. Outside we were greeted by a scene that I can only describe as utter devastation.

'Good grief!' I gasped.

I couldn't believe my eyes. Practically the whole of Tavistock Square apart from our little corner had been totally destroyed in the blast.

'The church is completely gone,' someone said.

It was now just a pile of rubble, and all the windows of the few buildings that were still standing had been blown out.

Looking around at the carnage, I knew we had been very lucky. It was a miracle that the windows in our rehearsal room had remained intact.

'It must have missed us by a whisker,' said Daphne.

It was scary to think how close we had all just come to being blown to smithereens and that we had just danced our way through it.

5

Ballet in the Blitz

Every night it was the same routine. As soon as it got dark the air-raid siren would go off as regular as clockwork. While I was at Italia Conti there were nightly bombings in London.

'Action stations, Rene,' boomed my grandfather's voice from downstairs as the loud, familiar wailing rang through the streets. 'Go and help Miss Smythe down from the attic.'

'All right, Papa,' I sighed.

Miss Smythe was the tiniest woman that I'd ever seen in my life; she was like a little bird with fluffy white hair that stuck up in a fuzzy halo around her head.

Instead of an Anderson shelter at the bottom of the garden like the one we'd had at our old house, my grandparents had a Morrison shelter in the dining-room. It was a big steel cage with a solid top that you could use as a table during the day and then climb underneath into the cage part during the bombings. It was a huge, ugly thing that almost took up the whole room, but at least it was warm and dry inside, and it was safer

83

than being out in the garden in a rickety Anderson shelter.

By the time I'd helped the frail spinster down three flights of stairs we could have been bombed to high heaven. But finally, we made it down to the dining-room.

'In you go,' I said as I gave her her a helpful push into the shelter.

'Thank you, dear,' she replied.

It was a bit of a squash with four of us all laid out in a row, and it wasn't very comfy. When the air-raid siren sounded really early on like tonight I got so bored cooped up in that metal cage with three old people. But suddenly I had a great idea.

'I know,' I said. 'I'll do a performance to cheer you all up.'

'Rene, I really don't think that's necessary,' sighed my grandmother wearily.

But I was all fired up after a day of singing and dancing at Italia Conti, and once I'd got a bee in my bonnet there was no stopping me. Every woman at that time wanted to look like the film star Jane Russell, and even though I was only twelve I was no exception. Much to my grandmother's disgust I took off my nightie, whipped off the scarf that she had around her neck, wrapped it round my non-existent boobies and started flouncing around like a Forties risqué glamour girl in just my vest and knickers.

'I know a fabulous Betty Grable number,'

I said, before launching into an enthusiastic rendition of 'I Heard the Birdies Sing'.

'I took one look at you and Cupid took a good swing,' I sang, failing to notice that the three OAPs who formed my audience were sitting there with a look of complete horror on their faces.

'Rene, I really don't think this is appropriate,' said my grandmother.

'Oh, Gaga, you're such a spoilsport,' I said. 'I've got another song I could do if you don't like that one.'

'Rene, that's enough,' said my grandfather sternly. 'You'll give poor Miss Smythe a heart attack.'

It was only then that I glanced over at the old woman and saw the shocked look on her face. I'm surprised she didn't have a stroke on the spot.

'I only wanted to try and cheer you all up while the bombs were coming down,' I grumbled.

As usual we spent all night in the shelter under the table, and then at 7 a.m. I climbed out and went and got myself ready. I pulled my hair into a bun, made sure that my dance bag was packed, and then stepped over the rubble of the previous night's bombings and headed to the Tube station. By now the war had just become part and parcel of my daily life.

My grandparents never showed any interest in my dancing and they never asked me anything about Italia Conti. There was no 'How was your day?' or 'What did you have for lunch?' I was left to get on with it, and that was what I got used to.

My grandmother would make an evening meal for me, although she was a dreadful cook. The pastry on her steak and kidney puddings was always as heavy as lead, and the filling was just as unappetising, with grey meat floating in a watery gravy. My grandfather would make himself useful around the house, and he'd boil up my washing in the big copper in the scullery and do the shopping every day.

In many ways he was a nicer, more approachable person that my grandmother, so it was him whom I asked to get me some sanitary towels when I started my periods.

'Papa, when you're out doing the shopping today, please could you bring me some sanitary towels from the chemist?' I said, my cheeks turning red.

Even though he was very Victorian in some of his attitudes, he wasn't the least bit embarrassed.

'Yes, all right, dear,' he said. 'I'll get you your women's things.'

I think the reason he was always so keen to do the shopping was that it was an excuse to stop in every pub on the way home and have a few pints of ale. That day, when I came home from Italia Conti, there was no sign of my grandfather.

'Where's Papa?' I asked my grandmother.

'No idea,' she sighed. 'He went off to do the shopping and I haven't seen hide nor hair of him since.'

By 10 p.m. I was starting to get worried. But Grandmother went to the front door before going to bed, and suddenly I heard the door open and then a terrible thud.

'Good grief, Henry!' I heard her yell.

I ran out into the hallway and there was Papa sprawled out face down on the tiled floor.

'Look who I found asleep on the doorstep worse for wear,' she tutted. 'He must have nodded off stood up with his head resting on the door, because when I opened it he fell straight in.'

Gaga was certainly not amused.

'Are you all right, Papa?' I asked, trying to pull him up.

'I'm fine, Rene. And don't you worry, I've got your women's things,' he beamed, handing me a large packet of sanitary towels.

But for the most part I dealt with things on my own, and there were only a few times that it bothered me. One of those was at the end of my first year at Italia Conti when the school put on its annual production of *Where the Rainbow Ends*. It was a very famous play about a group of children who have to rescue their parents and face lots of dangers on the way. In the end they're helped by St George, and it's all very English and patriotic.

'It's going to be at the Coliseum,' said Tony excitedly. ''Ere, imagine that, Rene. Us lot prancing round on one of the West End's biggest stages.'

'And in front of the King,' said Daphne.

I couldn't believe that we would be doing a Royal Command Performance for King George and Queen Elizabeth. I was even more thrilled when I was given a brief solo to perform.

'Irene, I'd like you to be the evil blue fairy,' Miss Moira the ballet teacher told me. 'It's your job to flit from one side of the stage to the other. Do you think you can do that, dear?'

'Yes, Miss Moira,' I said.

I was even more chuffed when I saw my costume – a blue dress with a boned bodice and a skirt with floaty bits of fabric coming off it.

But my heart was in my mouth as I turned up to rehearsals. With over 2,300 seats, the Coliseum was the biggest theatre in the West End and I was completely overwhelmed.

'This place is huge,' I sighed as I stood on the eighty-foot stage and stared out at all the seats. 'It's going to take me all day to dance across this stage.'

It seemed to go on for ever, and there was

a huge, ornate domed roof and marble pillars.

We were thrown in at the deep end, as we were expected to learn the routine in half a day and we only had a week of rehearsals.

'At the end of the performance the whole cast will come back on stage, and you must all turn stage right and curtsey to the royal box,' Toni Shanley told us. 'But there must be no staring, and under no circumstances must you look directly at the King and Queen, as that would be a breach of royal protocol. Please cast your eyes downward.

'Is that clear?'

'Yes, Miss Toni,' we all replied.

I was fascinated by the whole idea of the royal family.

'Do you think they'll just use the normal theatre toilets like everyone else?' I asked Tony Newley.

'Oh, Irene, don't be silly,' he said. 'They're royalty. They don't go to the lav.'

I was so naïve that I didn't realise he was joking, and for many years afterwards I still believed that the royal family were too posh to go to the toilet!

Soon it was the night of the big performance. As I waited in the wings for my turn to dance on stage I just felt tremendously excited rather than nervous.

'Blue fairy, on you go,' whispered Moira Shanley.

Right on cue I ran onto the stage. The bright lights dazzled me and I could only make out the first row of the audience as the rest of the auditorium just looked very black. I took a deep breath and forced myself to remember Miss Toni's words:

'Focus on the front row of the dress circle. That way you'll lift your head up, and the audience will see your eyes and the whole of your face. And smile, girls. Smile.'

As I danced across that stage I made sure that I had the biggest, broadest smile on my face. But the strange thing was, it wasn't forced or fake. I was genuinely happy, as I suddenly realised in that moment that my dream really had come true. Here I was, nearly ten years later, dancing like one of those fairies I'd seen in the pantomime at the Clapham Grand. Not only that, it was on the stage of the biggest theatre in the West End. Performing in front of that huge crowd gave me such a thrill.

'If only Mum were here to see me,' I thought to myself.

But there was no time to be sad, and soon I was curtseying to the King and Queen and basking in the audience's applause. Everyone was on a high and even strict Miss Toni seemed pleased with our performance.

'That was a job well done, everyone,' she said, although her face still didn't crack a smile.

I was still buzzing afterwards, and I didn't want to take off my fairy costume and get changed back into my ordinary clothes, as that would mean it was all over. As I got ready to go home I watched the rest of my classmates being greeted in the dressing-room by their proud parents, who had all come to watch the show.

'Oh, Daphne darling, you were absolutely wonderful,' said her mother, handing her a red rose and a huge box of chocolates.

Others were being lavished with hugs and kisses and praise for their performance. I knew there was no one in the audience who was there for me, but I hadn't expected there to be. As I squeezed my way out and headed to the Tube I refused to feel sorry for myself or let it get to me.

As part of your training at Italia Conti you were also sent off to appear in other productions during the school holidays. In the early Forties there were little variety theatres in every town and suburb, so there were endless opportunities to perform in summer seasons and pantomimes. I did a short tour with the Sadler's Wells Opera in which I played a gingerbread child in *Hansel and Gretel*, and I appeared in a variety show in Brighton. There were no such things as chaperones in those days. We just got on a train on our own and got on with it. A lot of the time we had to find our own places to stay.

When I was thirteen we were sent to work at a pantomime at the Theatre Royal in King's Lynn. Normally you wrote to the theatre where you were performing and they organised your digs, but our train was late into Norwich and by the time we got there that evening to speak to the stage manager it was all closed up.

'What are we going to do?' said my friend Ruth, who had been sent to perform in the show with me.

'Don't worry,' I told her. 'We'll just find somewhere ourselves.'

So we ended up walking up and down the streets, knocking on doors to see if we could find a bed for the night. But nobody had any room for the two of us, and as it got later and later we were getting more and more desperate. Then we knocked on the door of a terraced house and an old man opened it.

'We're dancers working at the local theatre and we're looking for somewhere to stay,' I told him. 'Do you think you might be so kind as to put us up for the night?'

'Well, I'm sure I could sort summink out for a couple of lovely young 'uns like you,' he said in his broad Norfolk accent.

He seemed like a nice, kindly man so we followed him into the house and he showed us his bedroom.

'You ladies can 'ave this room and I'll have forty winks downstairs,' he said, giving us a toothless grin.

Ruth and I looked at each other in horror. The place was absolutely filthy and everything was covered in a sheet of dust. His bedroom had a strange musty smell and the sheets looked like they hadn't been boiled up in the copper for years.

'What shall we do?' whispered Ruth when he went back downstairs. 'This place is revolting.'

'Beggars can't be choosers,' I said. 'It's getting late, and I don't fancy wandering up and down for hours in the dark.'

Even though his house was filthy he seemed like a nice old fellow, and he was letting us stay for free. But neither Ruth nor I got much sleep that night. We both slept fully dressed on top of the bedclothes and we even left our coats on. Bed bugs were very common in those days and I spent most of the night scratching. Neither of us could wait to leave in the morning.

'I feel so grubby,' said Ruth. 'Before we go to the theatre shall we go to the baths?'

Most towns and cities in the Forties had what were known as public baths. Sometimes our lodgings didn't have much hot water to go round or even a proper bath, so they were a godsend when we were working away from home doing a show.

When we walked in there was a woman sitting at a little kiosk.

'Ninepence for a first-class ticket or six-pence for second,' she told us.

The only difference was that with the first-class ones you got two towels and a scoop of bath salts, and with the second-class ones you only got one towel.

'Second will be fine,' I said.

It was expensive enough for us as it was.

She handed us both a meagre piece of soap that had been cut from a big block. Soap was rationed during the war and you couldn't get any nice, sweet-smelling ones, just this rock-hard green stuff that didn't lather up no matter how hard you scrubbed. Shampoo wasn't available either, so you had to use the same soap if you wanted to give your hair a wash, but I'd stopped doing that after I'd discovered how badly it stung my eyes.

'I can't wait to feel clean again,' said Ruth as we went upstairs and sat on the second-class bench until the numbers on our tickets were called.

'I know what you mean,' I replied. 'I still feel all itchy and I'm sure I heard rats scurrying around last night.'

I didn't mind waiting in the public baths as it was all steamy and warm in there, and you could hear the sound of people singing echoing around the tiled walls. Finally it was our turn and an attendant showed me to my cubicle. It had a stone floor and a huge iron roll-top bath with copper taps but no plug in it.

'Give me a shout when you've finished, love, and I'll empty out the water for you,' the attendant told me.

I suppose it was like that to stop anyone from running endless baths. It felt wonderful sinking into the piping hot water after spending the night in that filthy bed. After I'd got out I washed my clothes and underwear in the bathwater, and then got changed into some clean things. Whenever I went to the public baths I would always bring my dirty washing with me.

'Thank you,' I said to the attendant.

She went in and opened the tap to let the water out. It was also her job to collect any leftover pieces of soap. These would be melted down and made into a new block, although the thought of that always made me cringe a bit.

'Ahh, that's better,' sighed Ruth. 'I feel clean again.'

'Now we'd better go and report in with the theatre,' I said.

The stage manager was very apologetic about the mix-up with our lodgings.

'Don't worry,' he said. 'We've got you somewhere to stay. You won't have to go wandering the streets again tonight.'

After morning rehearsals were over we went to get some lunch at the local British

Restaurant. These were communal kitchens set up in towns and cities during the war, to feed people who'd been bombed out of their houses or had run out of ration coupons, or just people like us who needed a cheap feed. For ninepence you could get a basic meal, such as a bowl of soup or a steaming plate of stew. Afterwards we traipsed round to our new digs, which was a big Victorian terrace house.

'This looks a bit better,' said Ruth.

We knocked on the door and a middle-aged woman and a girl in her twenties who I assumed was her daughter answered it. They were both wearing pink satin dressing-gowns, which I thought was a bit odd as it was the middle of the afternoon.

'Hello,' I said. 'The theatre sent us. They said you could put us up while we're doing the panto.'

'Oh, er, yes, dear,' she said. 'You're the theatricals, are you? Come on in.'

An American army officer in uniform was standing in the hallway.

'Hi, gals,' he grinned. 'Are you the new recruits?'

'Oi, you, keep yer mouth shut,' the woman said in a hushed voice, ushering him away. 'They're two nice young ladies from the theatre. You keep yer 'ands off.'

She took us up to our room on the first floor. It was a six-bedroom house but, looking through the doors as we walked past, we noticed that all of the bedrooms seemed to have been split into two.

'Why do two women need a twelve-bedroom house?' I asked Ruth.

We soon found out. Every fifteen minutes or so the front doorbell would ring and we'd hear the sound of people traipsing up and down the stairs. They were up and down all afternoon and into the evening.

'Who are all these callers and what are they doing?' I said, puzzled.

Ruth and I peeped through the keyhole, and every once in a while an American soldier would walk past arm in arm with a pretty woman wearing nothing but a lacy dressing-gown.

'Oh, my giddy aunt,' said Ruth. 'I think I know what this place is, Irene. It's a knocking shop.'

'What do you mean?' I asked.

'It's a brothel,' she replied. 'For the Yanks.'

I was very shocked when she explained what that meant. I might have been streetwise, but I was still very green in some respects. I'd heard that these places existed but I was completely terrified.

'Give me that chair, Ruth, and I'll barricade the door,' I said. 'I don't want any of those GIs losing their way and wandering into our bedroom by mistake.'

'Perish the thought,' she said.

We were both absolutely petrified. Ruth and I slept in the same bed, and we spent all night clinging on to each other. We couldn't get out of there quickly enough the next morning.

'You sent us to a brothel,' Ruth told the stage manager when we got to the theatre. 'We can't stay there.'

Once again he was full of apologies.

'I'm dreadfully sorry, there's obviously been another mix-up,' he said. 'We didn't realise what type of place it was.'

Thankfully at last we were sent to a proper boarding house, where we stayed for the month that the panto was on, but I vowed never to go to Norfolk again!

I was so naïve in those days, and as for boys, I didn't have a clue. I wasn't as glamorous as some of the other girls at Italia Conti. I didn't wear any make-up, and I was a funny little thing with skinny legs and two long plaits.

But I did have a bit of a crush on one of the dancers in the King's Lynn panto, who was tall and blond.

'Isn't Malcolm lovely?' I sighed to Ruth. 'He's like a Greek god.'

'Oh, don't waste your time admiring him,' she said. 'He's a queen.'

'What do you mean,' I gasped. 'Is he royal?'

She just rolled her eyes at me and laughed.

'For God's sake, Irene, where have you come from?'

'I really don't know what you mean,' I said.

For someone so streetwise and independent, I really was quite ignorant when it came to matters of the opposite sex.

After I'd been at Italia Conti for a couple of years the school moved out of Tavistock Square. Miss Conti had found a permanent home for it in Archer Street, just off Shaftesbury Avenue. The only drawback about this new location was that it was slap-bang in the middle of London's red-light district. It was directly behind the Windmill Theatre, famous for its nude shows and 'we never close' slogan. As I walked down Archer Street on my way to class in the morning, a lot of the doorways would be open and I'd see men disappearing up the carpeted stairways with their bare light bulbs.

No one had ever sat down and told me about the birds and the bees, but I learned what I could from playground gossip and talking to friends. One day at Italia Conti I could see a big group of pupils gathered round in a corner of the corridor looking at something.

'Come and have a gander at this, Rene,' shouted Tony Newley.

Out of curiosity I went to see what they were all so interested in. Much to my horror it was some black-and-white photos of men and women with their clothes off doing all sorts of odd things.

'Eurgh!' I shrieked. 'How disgusting.'

Then I ran away and all the boys laughed.

A lot of the older girls had boyfriends, but I just wasn't interested. Daphne, who was a year older than me and was 15 by now, was very beautiful and she was always getting asked out by American soldiers.

'I got chatting to a GI on the train last week and he invited me to one of their big do's in the West End,' she told me.

After classes that day I helped her get dressed into the amazing ball gown that her mother had made her. It was white satin, and her mum had spent hours sewing all these tiny crystals onto the skirt by hand. It was so big she could hardly move in it.

'You look stunning, Daphne,' I said. 'I can help you onto the Tube if you want.'

'Thank you, Irene,' she said. 'I wish you were coming with me.'

But even though I was fascinated, I was glad that I wasn't going. I had no desire to go out with an American GI, and even if I had I knew that I would have been completely out of my depth. I had lots of boys as friends, but I wouldn't dream of flirting with anybody.

In May 1945 a group of us from Italia Conti were sent to do a show up in Rochdale. We got the train there and it was packed with soldiers. They all looked very tired and had their rifles and kitbags with them, and it was a job for us to squeeze into the carriages.

'I wonder why so many of them are coming back from the war now?' I said.

We soon found out. A few days later we did a matinée performance, and as we walked out of the stage door and into a cobbled square we got a shock. The whole place was packed with people, and they were singing and dancing and waving Union flags.

'What the blinking heck's going on?' gasped Daphne.

'Haven't you heard?' said a woman skipping past. 'The war's over.'

None of us could believe it. We didn't know a thing about it and we'd been performing in the theatre when Winston Churchill had made his big announcement on the wireless. Now we'd come out to chaos and we were completely overwhelmed.

A young boy ran over to me.

'It's the end of the war,' he shouted over the din. 'Can I give you a kiss?'

'No, you bloomin' well can't,' I told him.

The war might have ended but I wasn't going to let him put one past me.

'Oh, Rene, don't be so rotten,' said Daphne.

Looking back now, it was probably very mean of me.

Suddenly we got pulled into a big circle, and soon we were all laughing and joking and dancing around. It took a while for the enormity of the news to sink in, but when it did I realised that the end of the war meant one very important thing. My mum and my brother could finally come home, and our family would be reunited at last.

6

Treading the Boards

I couldn't wait for Mum to come home, but what I wasn't expecting was for her to bring her new boyfriend back with her.

I knew she'd met someone in Egypt, as she had told me so in a letter.

I've been spending time with a cellist called Harry. He's a very fine musician and has been married before a long time ago. I really think you would like him, Rene.

But I hadn't expected that he would move in with us at my grandparents' house. I'm not sure what Gaga and Papa thought about the idea of them living together under their roof when they weren't married, as they never said. Although I was happy for my mother, as I knew how lonely she'd been since my father had died, I was apprehensive about meeting this new man in her life. When she was at home I was used to being the sole focus of her affections, and I knew it was going to be strange having to share her with someone else, especially when we'd been apart for so long.

I wasn't exactly sure when Mum was due back, but one day I came home from class and saw some bags in the hallway.

Then I saw her violin case at the bottom of the stairs and my heart soared.

She was home.

'Mum?' I shouted, running upstairs to our sitting-room on the second floor. 'Mum, where are you?'

She came out onto the landing to greet me.

'Oh, Rene, dear,' she smiled.

I threw my arms around her and smelled that familiar flowery scent of the shampoo called Drene that she used.

'I'm so glad that you're home,' I said. 'I've missed you.'

She didn't say much but when we pulled apart I could see the tears in her eyes. I'd been so excited and overcome that I hadn't noticed the man lurking awkwardly in the doorway behind us.

'Oh, Rene, this is Harry,' said Mum, introducing us.

He was a tall, strong-looking bloke with wispy grey hair, in his late thirties like my mother.

'Hello,' I said. 'Pleased to meet you.'

'Likewise,' he said, shaking my hand. 'Kitty's told me a lot about you.'

It all felt very formal and awkward having this stranger around the house. Harry wasn't what I would call a handsome man, but he and my mother seemed to get on well and I could see that they shared a passion for music. Music was my mother's life and Harry had played in all of the major philharmonic orchestras. They soon found work, and they would practise for hours together during the day, doing duets with their cello and violin, and then go off and perform at night.

I'd spent my whole life longing for a father figure, but I was 15 and I had no intention of having one now. Even though I loved having Mum home again I was still very independent, and I was either out at Italia Conti during the day or away performing in shows. I'd had to become very self-reliant and make my own decisions when Mum was away, and that just continued. But when I was at home she liked to make a fuss of me.

'Would you like a cheese sandwich, Rene?' she asked me one day.

'Please could I have a boiled egg for my tea instead?'

'You and your boiled eggs,' she smiled. 'Of course you can, dear.'

When she brought it up to our living-room

on the second floor on a silver tray and cut the top off for me, I could see Harry rolling his eyes and tutting.

'You spoil that girl,' I heard him grumbling to Mum later on.

'Oh, don't be so silly,' she told him. 'Rene's my daughter. It's nice to be able to look after her after being away for so long.'

I think Harry was very jealous and resentful of how close Mum and I were, and he didn't like it if he wasn't the centre of attention. Looking back now, I think how childish that was of him to feel threatened by a teenager. In one sense he was not at all the type of person that I thought my mother would settle down with. He used to gamble on the horses and Mum would get very cross with him as he was always losing money. But I think ultimately it was their passion for music that bound them together.

It felt strange having a man in the house. My brother Raymond was so much older than me that he'd hardly lived at home when I had, and my grandfather was in his eighties. I'd always felt that I'd missed out growing up without a father, but I certainly didn't want Harry to fill that gap. He and I were never close, even though my mother was with him right up until he died in his seventies. They never got married, but I think that most people assumed they were.

Raymond had also come back to London

after the war and he was now working as a schoolteacher in the East End. He married a fellow teacher called Evelyn and they had a little girl called Linda. He wasn't keen on Harry either, although I don't think anyone could ever have matched up to our father in his eyes.

'I don't know why she's with that man,' he used to say. 'He's not good enough for Mother.'

Raymond rented a house around the corner from my grandparents in Battersea so he would often pop in. I loved to sit and listen to his stories about the children he taught in the East End. The area had been badly bombed during the war and he was shocked by the poverty.

'In winter the poor kids are sewn into their clothes,' he said. 'Their parents rub goose fat on the insides of their vests and they're stitched in.'

He told me how some children were even encased in a layer of brown paper next to their skin to try to keep out the cold.

'They must be filthy by the time it's spring,' I said.

I knew Mum had always struggled for money, but at least I'd had what was known as a liberty vest – a little waistcoat lined with wool that I wore under my clothes to keep warm. Hearing Raymond's stories made me realise that I'd had it lucky in some respects.

A few months after the war ended it was time for me to leave Italia Conti. I'd been there three years by that point, and several of my friends had already left and started working. Tony Newley, as we'd all expected, had soon made a name for himself by winning the title role in a children's film called *Dusty Bates*, followed by that of the Artful Dodger in David Lean's film of *Oliver Twist*, while Nanette was hoping to be an actress and Daphne, who was due to leave, wanted to be a singer.

You didn't take exams in ballet or dance in those days, but I did have to do an exam in elocution. It was preying on my mind, as occasionally when I was under pressure my stammer would come back. But even the dragon-like Miss Margaret was understanding about it.

'I know you're worried that you will stammer, dear, so I've arranged for you to do yours one-to-one with an examiner rather than with everyone else.'

'Thank you, Miss Margaret,' I said. 'I'm really grateful.'

I felt sick with nerves as I walked into the room, where the examiner sat behind a desk.

'Hello, Miss Starr,' she said. 'When you're ready please begin.'

I had to recite the poem 'I Wandered Lonely as a Cloud' by Wordsworth. Because

I was nervous I did begin to stutter slightly, but I was determined I was going to do it.

'I'd like to start again if I may,' I asked her.

'Very well,' she said. 'Just take your time.'

'I wandered l-lonely as a cloud/That floats on high o'er v-vales and hills...'

I still stammered on the odd word here and there, but I got through it and made sure that I pronounced every word properly. I couldn't believe it when Miss Margaret came out later to give me my results.

'I got a merit?' I gasped.

'Well done, Irene,' she said. 'That's a real achievement.'

I couldn't believe it and I was so proud of myself. After stammering very badly for most of my life until then, having a certificate in elocution was really important to me. I knew my career was never going to be in acting, and the stammer didn't affect my dancing or singing, but it meant a lot nonetheless.

When the time came for pupils to leave they were sent out to several auditions on their own to see how they fared. My first one was for a part in the chorus line of a musical called *High Button Shoes* at the Hippodrome in Leicester Square.

'I want you to go for this, Irene,' said Miss Conti. 'I don't think you'll get it, but it will be good practice for you.'

'I'll do my best,' I told her.

I was crippled with nerves when I turned

up at the theatre on the day of the audition. There was a long line of girls already there, and they all seemed so much older and more sophisticated than me with their red lipstick, curled hair and high heels. I didn't wear a scrap of make-up and still looked about twelve.

'Here's your number,' said a woman going down the queue with a clipboard. 'Please wait at the side of the stage.'

The auditorium was very dark and the stage was enormous. I couldn't even see who was auditioning me as I walked out. I went over to the pianist and gave her my music, and then took my position in the spotlight.

'What are you going to sing for us today?' a man's voice boomed out of the darkness.

'"Alice Blue Gown",' I said.

'Start when you're ready, dear.'

'All right then.'

My heart was racing so much I could almost hear the blood whooshing in my ears as I started my song and dance routine.

After I'd finished it was so quiet you could have heard a pin drop.

'Thank you,' said the mystery voice, 'We'll let you know.'

'Next, please.'

I knew instantly that I hadn't got it, otherwise they would have told me to wait behind or asked me for a callback, which is when they narrow it down and select certain people to come back for a second audition. In a way it was almost a relief, as the whole experience had terrified me.

Looking back, I'm not surprised I didn't get a part, as I was so green and there was nothing sophisticated or glamorous about me in those days. One person who did have a successful audition that day, though, was an unknown dancer called Audrey Heburn, who went on to appear in the chorus line of the musical.

'You were right, I didn't get it,' I told Miss Conti when I got back to school.

'Don't be downcast, dear,' she told me. 'Life in the theatre is full of ups and downs. You have to get used to being rejected and develop a thick skin.'

I knew I had to learn to accept that I wasn't going to get every job that I went for.

A few weeks later a handful of us were sent for an audition for a summer season in a variety show in Blackpool.

'Look on this as another practice run,' Miss Conti told us. 'I'm not expecting any of you to get it. Just learn from the experience.'

It was at a rehearsal room in central London, and when the women auditioning us told us that it involved a lot of ballet I started to think that perhaps I was in with a chance. We each did a song and then a dance routine, and afterwards she came and tapped me on the shoulder.

'I think we could use a lovely little dancer like you,' she said.

Out of all of us that had gone from Italia Conti, I was the only one to have got it. I was over the moon and I was grinning from ear to ear when I went home that night.

'I've got a job,' I told Mum. 'I'm going to Blackpool.'

'Well, it's not quite the West End but it's a start,' she smiled.

It meant a lot to me because it was the first job that I'd got independently from Italia Conti through my own talent.

So, after three happy years, it meant my time had come to leave the school. There was no fancy leaving ceremony or graduation. A diploma in musical theatre was shoved in my hand and I was sent on my merry way.

'I'm so sad to leave,' I told Daphne. 'I've been really happy here.'

'You'll be fine, Irene,' she said. 'I'll miss you.'

I couldn't resist taking a last walk around one of the rehearsal rooms before I left. I looked at the bare walls, the wooden floor, the huge mirrors, the long ballet barre and the piano in the corner. There was nothing fancy about any of it, but it had been my world, my little haven and my very own fairyland. The time I'd spent at Italia Conti had taken me away from the harsh reality of the outside world, the war and missing

Mum. I was never happier than when I was in one of these rooms doing a dance class.

'Good luck, Irene,' said Miss Conti as I walked out of the building. 'I hope you have a long and lustrous career on the stage.'

'Thank you,' I smiled. 'Thank you for everything.'

Even though I was sad to leave, another part of me couldn't wait to get started. I'd already had a taste of what life was like on the stage, and I just wanted to get out there and perform. I wanted the lovely costumes, the glamour and the lights. I liked the feeling of being different to everyone else, and the excitement and incredible buzz you felt before a show.

I was ready. Soon my bag was packed and I was on a train up to Blackpool. It was a long summer season lasting twenty weeks from April to September. In those days Blackpool was the entertainment capital of the North. Every summer thousands of holidaymakers flocked there and there were several theatres that attracted some of the country's biggest stars.

I was going to be performing in a variety show in a little theatre at the end of the North Pier. There were six of us in the show and we'd been billeted to a theatrical boarding house run by a lady called Mrs Bloom. She opened the door to me in her housecoat and slippers, and she had curlers in her hair covered with a scarf tied up like a turban.

'Come in, lass,' she said in her strong Lancashire accent. 'I'll take yer 'at for yer.'

As I walked in the door a horrible stench hit my nostrils. 'It's your looky day, luv, you're just in time for tea,' she said. The other girls were already sitting around the table and I smiled at them politely.

'I thought you girls might like to try a Lancashire delicacy,' she said, plonking a plate of steaming white stuff in front of us.

'It's tripe and onions boiled in milk. I've been slaving over a hot stove all day, so I hope you like it.'

I'd never eaten tripe before but I knew it was the lining of a cow's stomach. It looked absolutely disgusting and it stank to high heaven.

Mrs Bloom stared at us expectantly.

'Don't be polite,' she smiled. 'Tuck in, girls. You dancers need to keep yer strength up.'

She looked so proud of it that I thought I'd better show willing and I cautiously took one tiny mouthful. But as soon as the flabby white stuff hit my throat I retched.

'I'm dreadfully sorry,' I said, pushing my plate away, 'but I don't think I can eat this.'

'Me neither,' said one of the other girls, putting her knife and fork down. 'I'm from Lancashire but I can't stand the stuff myself.'

Meanwhile the other girls looked like they were about to be sick.

Mrs Bloom looked devastated and she burst into floods of dramatic tears.

'I don't bloomin' believe it,' she sobbed. 'I've been slaving away all day to make that for you lot and this is how you thank me.'

Then we all started to cry too, because we felt so guilty. She was crying ... now we were all crying. It was certainly a memorable first night in Blackpool!

'I suppose I'd better get yer all a tongue sandwich then instead,' she sighed, dabbing her eyes with a hankie as she shuffled off to the kitchen.

'I feel terrible about upsetting her,' said one of the girls. 'I'm Gracie by the way.'

We all introduced ourselves. The other girls were Gracie, Edith, Valerie, Ethel and Mary. They were all from the North and had been to stage school like me.

'This is my first job,' I told them.

'It'll be reet hard work,' said Ethel. 'Summer seasons always are.'

She was right. Every day we did a matinée and two evening shows. We had three different shows to learn and it changed around every three weeks. We got paid £30 a week, which was a good wage in those days. After I'd paid my board to Mrs Bloom, I always sent some money home to Mum for my keep as I knew it was still a struggle for her to find regular work.

We were part of a cast of eccentric characters who did the rounds of the variety shows around the country. Like the comedian who chain-smoked a hundred cigarettes a day.

'You can always tell when he's coming as you can smell the tobacco before you see him,' said Ethel.

He smoked so much he was practically yellow from top to toe and we nicknamed him Mr Nicotine.

The poor fellow came into the theatre one day looking very glum.

'What's the matter with you?' asked Mary.

'The doc says I've got to give up smoking or I'll be dead in a week,' he wheezed.

'Good grief,' said Valerie. 'Well, I suppose you always are puffing away.'

'He told me to suck peppermints to take my mind off the cigarettes,' he said, and from then on he must have sucked hundreds of mints a day.

Top of the bill was a famous comedian called Sandy Powell, who was known for his catchphrase 'Can you hear me, Mother?'

In between shows there was only enough time to have a quick sunbathe in a deck chair or go and play on the arcades on the pier.

'I love Blackpool,' said Ethel. 'It's so much fun.'

One afternoon we went for a walk along

115

the promenade that was known as the Golden Mile.

'Crikey, you can hardly see the sand for all the crowds,' I said.

Thousands of people were crammed together on the beach like sardines and there wasn't an inch of space. There were children having donkey rides, and men in suits sunbathing with their trousers rolled up and knotted hankies on their heads. I'd never seen anything like it. Everywhere was packed, from the souvenir shops that sold cheeky postcards, sticks of rock and 'kiss me quick' hats to the fish and chip shops.

It only cost sixpence to see the variety show and every night we played to a packed house of holidaymakers. Families would sit there nibbling on candy-floss and crunching toffee apples while we did our ballet dancing. It was very different to the sophisticated audiences in the big London theatres.

One night we came out of the stage door and there was a small group of teenage boys waiting for us. One of them stepped forward as Gracie walked past.

'I loved your dancing, Miss, and I got you these,' he said, handing her a box of chocolates.

'Thank you,' she said. 'I shall share them with my friends. But I can't stop and chat, I'm afraid,' she told him as she walked off with her nose in the air to catch up with us.

We were all giggling as we jumped straight onto the tram that ran all the way down the sea front and would take us back to our lodgings.

'I think you've got yourself an admirer there,' I teased.

Grace was short, blonde and extremely pretty, and she knew it too.

'I like older men,' she said. 'Talking of which, are we going out dancing tomorrow night?'

Normally after three shows a day we were exhausted, but we'd heard Ted Heath's big band were playing in the Tower Ballroom.

'One of the trumpet players has apparently got a bit of a crush on me,' smiled Grace.

So the next night after work we went jiving. It was gone 1 a.m. before we walked back to our digs arm in arm.

'Do you think Mrs Bloom will have waited up for us?' whispered Ethel.

Thankfully we had our own key, but sweetly she'd left out a sandwich for each of us and some cocoa.

'At least it's not tripe,' laughed Mary.

Blackpool had been a lot of fun but then it was back to London in the autumn. I wasn't worried about my next job as there was plenty of work around in those days and I was never unemployed for long. Every Tuesday I got *The Stage* newspaper, where all the jobs were listed, and then I'd go along and audition for anything that took my fancy. If I was out of work it would only be for a week or two, and I was allowed to go and sign on.

One week I saw an interesting advert saying, 'Madam Walker's Academy of Girls needs dancers.' I decided to go along for the audition.

I'd heard of Madam Walker before. She was an elderly lady who'd been in the business all her life. She was a very fine singer but her grandfather wouldn't let her leave home to perform. Instead he'd built a studio for her in their garden in Portsmouth where she'd started an academy. By the 1940s she had over seventeen acts available for booking in theatres around the country. Her daughter Peggy worked with her and helped choreograph some of her routines.

'Well hello, darling,' she said to me in a very exaggerated posh voice. 'Tell me, what are you going to perform for me today?'

She was clutching a shawl around her shoulders and she had bright red lipstick on that was smeared over her teeth when she smiled. She was a real stager, which was how people referred to someone who had been in the business for years.

I did my routine for her and she gave me a big clap.

'Bravo!' she shouted. 'Marvellous, dear. I would like to send you down to my troupe at the Theatre Royal in Exeter to do some pantomimes.'

So I spent the next few months there appearing in *Mother Goose* and *Aladdin*. I enjoyed doing pantos, as there was always quite a bit of ballet in them. There was one scene in *Aladdin* where the hero went into the cave, and we had to pretend to be jewels and dance around.

The man playing Aladdin was a strapping, six-foot fellow, and he had to do a leap from the side of the stage and all of us dancers had to catch him and hold him up in the air. He was a big, muscular bloke and every night I lived in fear of dropping him.

'Be careful where you put your hands, girls,' I joked, as I was always worried about grabbing him on the jock strap by mistake!

We worked quite closely and intimately together every day, so you soon got to know people. We all had to get on and be nice to each other, because if you didn't then you'd be out of the door. In Exeter I became very friendly with one of the other dancers, who was called Shirley. She had a fantastic singing voice and became famous in the Fifties and Sixties as part of an act called the Kaye Sisters.

I got used to life on the road but it was always nice to work a bit closer to home, so I was pleased when I got a job as a dancer in *Dick Whittington* at the Bedford Theatre,

Camden Town. It was a very run-down, grotty little theatre with tiny dressing-rooms and a rat problem, but I still loved it. There was a certain charm about those old Victorian theatres and it was all a learning curve for me.

I was one of the peasant girls and I wore a blouse with puff sleeves, a waistcoat and a little skirt with ribbons and flowers in my hair. I could tell from the minute the curtain went up on the first night that they were going to be a lively crowd.

'I think they've all been to the public house on the way here,' one of the other girls whispered to me.

As we performed our opening dance the audience started whistling and cheering, and they were very rowdy. Unfortunately they seemed to take an instant dislike to the principal boy. This part in a panto was traditionally played by a beautiful young woman, but our principal boy was quite a large lady who was in her forties. We'd just finished our opening number and she was marching about the stage in front of us, slapping her thighs, when the audience started booing and jeering.

'Rubbish!' someone shouted.

'Get her off!' another voice said.

We weren't used to that kind of behaviour and we looked at each other in a panic.

'What's their problem?' I whispered to the

girl next to me.

'I don't think she's pretty enough for them,' she said.

Then suddenly, out of the corner of my eye, I saw something fly through the air and land on the stage right next to me. I looked down at the red, mushy mess.

'Jesus Christ, they're throwing rotten tomatoes at us,' I said.

'Not at us,' said another girl. 'At her.'

It was like something out of Shakespearean times. Much to her surprise, the poor principal boy was being pelted with rotten tomatoes. But, ever the professional, she completely ignored it and carried on with her lines regardless of the tomatoes splattering on her costume and around her feet.

'Carry on, girls,' the stage manager whispered from the wings.

But as we danced it was tricky not to slip on the rotten tomatoes squishing under our feet and a few poor girls went flying. The stage was absolutely covered and it was such a relief when the curtain came down between acts. But the principal boy didn't seem in the least bit bothered by her run-in with the audience.

'Well, it's a bit of a rum crowd in tonight,' she said, wiping squashed tomatoes off her shoes.

She didn't say another word about it. As we

say in the business, the show must go on, and it did. Thankfully the audience had calmed down by the second half. Rotten fruit aside, I loved doing pantomimes and summer seasons. But things were about to get a lot more glamorous for me.

7

Briefly a Bluebell

As soon as I opened the front door I could see my friend Audrey had something important to tell me.

'You look fit to burst,' I laughed. 'What is it?'

'Can I come in, Irene?' she asked. 'I'm on a break between seasons and I've got some news about a job I think you'd be interested in.'

I wasn't working at the time – I was 'resting', as we dancers liked to call it when we were in between jobs.

'That sounds exciting,' I said.

Audrey Hood was a very striking-looking auburn-haired girl who lived round the corner from me in Battersea. We'd become friends after getting the Tube home together from various auditions. I hadn't seen her for ages because for the past few months she'd been working as a Bluebell Girl in Germany. The Bluebells were a famous troupe known for their long-legged, beautiful girls, and they danced in glamorous theatres and nightclubs around the world.

'One of our Bluebells has only gone and got herself pregnant,' she told me, lowering her voice. 'She's had to leave very quickly and come back to England to get married.'

She explained that it meant her troupe were a girl short and the new season started in just over a week.

'I put in a good word for you with Miss Bluebell and told her what a lovely dancer you were, and guess what?' she said. 'She wants me to bring you back with me to Germany later this week.'

'Germany?' I gasped. 'But I've never even been abroad before.'

'It's a beautiful little ski resort in the Alps and you'll be dancing in a nightclub for the American soldiers.

'You should see them in their uniforms, Rene. Talk about handsome,' she said, giving me a wink.

'Hmmm, I'm not sure it's really my thing,' I told her.

'But it's a troupe, Irene, and a famous one at that,' she said. 'You get all your travel, food and lodgings paid too.'

For most young dancers in the Forties,

joining a troupe was the ultimate ambition, as it gave you a guaranteed, well-paid job for several months. You weren't allowed to join one until you were seventeen, but I was finally eligible.

I'd enjoyed doing pantomimes and summer seasons, but I wasn't working, and the idea of regular work and a bit of stability for a few months was appealing.

'Please, Irene, come to Germany with me,' she begged.

I looked at Audrey's pleading face.

'Go on then, Aud,' I said. 'I'll give it a try.'

I was a bit reluctant because, in my eyes, the Bluebells were more like glamorous showgirls than proper dancers. They had troupes performing all over the world, but the original group were based at the Folies Bergère, a famous nightclub in Paris. They wore very revealing corseted costumes, and often only had a few feathers and jewels to cover their modesty.

'There's nothing sleazy about it, you know,' said Audrey, reading my mind. 'It's all done very tastefully and modestly.'

'I know,' I said.

'You'd better pack your bags, then,' she said, giving me a hug.

'Miss Bluebell's going to be so pleased when I bring a pretty little treasure like you back with me, and it will be nice to have a bit of company on the journey out there.'

It was certainly going to be an adventure, that's for sure.

The Bluebells had a reputation for being very beautiful and glamorous, and thankfully I'd grown up a lot in the last two years since I'd left Italia Conti. I'd started wearing make-up, and my thick brown hair was now shoulder-length and every night I patiently put it in pin curls.

Two days later I was all packed and ready to go. My mother and Harry had gone on tour with an orchestra, and my grandparents as usual were totally uninterested in what I was doing.

'Bye, then. I'm off to Germany now,' I yelled.

I could have been popping out to the shops for all the reaction I got. I'd worn my winter coat as I thought it might be a bit chilly up in the Alps, and put on my gold clip-on earrings and lots of red lipstick in the hope that I looked glamorous enough. Audrey explained that we were heading to a place called Garmisch-Partenkirchen.

'It's a little town in the mountains in southern Germany near the border with Austria,' she said.

'I can't even pronounce it, never mind know where it is,' I told her.

It was a horrendous journey and it seemed to take us forever to get there. We had to get a coach to Dover, the ferry to Calais and then a train to Paris, where we eventually picked up another train that would take us across France and through Germany.

'I can see why you wanted a bit of company,' I told Audrey.

I was exhausted by the time we got off at the main station in Garmisch. But we still weren't quite there yet and I couldn't believe it when we had to take a rickety little railroad up to the top of a mountain.

'Isn't it beautiful?' said Audrey as we climbed higher up into the Alps.

'It's, er, very white,' I said, looking at the deep snow everywhere.

I could see how it would be some people's idea of heaven, with the crisp mountain air, snow-capped fir trees and little wooden chalets. But all I was thinking was where was the nearest shop and how the heck was I going to walk in these shoes?

'Let's head to our digs and I'll introduce you to the other girls,' said Audrey.

I felt so foolish as I'd come totally unprepared for the weather. My woollen coat, which was fine for dashing around London and getting on and off the Underground, felt way too thin up here, and I was so cold I was shivering violently. My court shoes were lethal on the snow and as I walked up the steep, icy path, dragging my suitcase behind me, I was slipping and sliding all over the place.

'Why didn't you tell me it was going to be freezing?' I gasped. 'I'm going to break my bloomin' neck.'

'I'm sorry, Irene. I thought you knew that it would be snowy in the Alps,' said Audrey apologetically.

Finally we reached our lodgings, which turned out to be a charming wooden ski chalet. Audrey knocked on the front door.

'Just a quick word of warning about Miss Bluebell,' she whispered as we waited for someone to open it. 'Some people have refused to work for her because they say she's a bit of a tigress, but I've never had a problem with her.'

'Now you tell me,' I teased.

I wasn't worried really. In my experience all dance teachers were sticklers for discipline and had a very no-nonsense attitude, so that didn't bother me.

Finally a beautiful blonde girl who was extremely tall came to the door.

'Hello, Gertie,' Audrey said to her. 'This is my good friend Irene Starr, who's come to replace Alice.'

'Pleased to meet you,' I said.

But she just looked me up and down like I was something that she'd trodden on in the street.

'Oh,' she said. 'Come in.'

There were eight other girls sat in the living-room. None of them seemed that friendly or welcoming.

'How tall are you?' one of them asked me.

'Five foot six in my stockinged feet,' I replied.

I saw them raise an eyebrow at each other. They were all in their early twenties and a fair bit older than me, and they seemed to tower over me.

'Well, I'm only five foot eight,' said Audrey.

'Yes, and you're the shortest girl here, remember,' said Gertie. 'Your friend is going to stick out like a sore thumb in our line-up.'

I'd only just arrived but I'd already started to wonder why I'd even bothered to come out here in the first place.

'I'm sorry, Irene,' said Audrey that night as we settled into our room. 'I didn't even think about your height. Let's see what Miss Bluebell says at rehearsals tomorrow.'

The following day we headed to the night-club where we'd be performing the nightly show. It was a prefab that had been built specially for the GIs stationed at the American base in Garmisch. The war had ended three years ago but they were still billeted there, helping to restore law and order in Germany.

As it was the start of the new season Miss Bluebell was waiting there to greet us. I'd been expecting someone very glamorous, but she was quite an ordinary-looking woman in her late thirties with a Scouse accent. Her real name was Margaret Kelly, but she'd been nicknamed Bluebell as a child because of the striking colour of her eyes, which were a very clear blue. She'd been a dancer, and was working in Paris in 1932 when she'd decided to form her own troupe.

'Hello, Miss Starr,' she said, shaking my hand. 'I trust you had a good journey?'

'It took us a while but we're here now,' I said.

'This is my husband, Marcel Leibovici,' she said, introducing me to a short, tubby man with dark hair. 'He deals with the business side of things.'

Miss Bluebell was well known in the industry and Audrey had filled me in on her story during our long journey to Germany.

'Marcel was a pianist and composer at the Folies Bergère, where they fell in love,' she'd said. 'He's a Romanian Jew, and during the war he was arrested and sent to a concentration camp. But the French Resistance helped him to escape and for the rest of the war Miss Bluebell hid him in Paris.

'Imagine that!' Audrey had sighed. 'Every day she risked her life and the lives of her four children to bring him food and drink. She was even interrogated by the Gestapo, you know, but she managed not to give anything away.'

She sounded like an incredible woman, and I was keen to impress her.

As we started rehearsals, she watched us with her hawk-like eyes and I didn't dare put a foot wrong.

'Well, I think you're a fine dancer, Miss Starr,' she told me at the end of the day. 'I like girls with character as well as beauty and Audrey spoke very highly of you. But I'm afraid there appears to have been a bit of a misunderstanding. I suspect you're just too short for this particular troupe.'

'But I've come all this way,' I told her.

'I know it's not your fault, and I'm keen to try and make it work,' she said. 'Why don't you carry on rehearsing with the girls, and I'll come back at the end of the week and see how you're getting on?'

'The only other thing I need to tell you, Miss Starr, is that I run a respectable troupe and the only way you can get respect is by behaving.'

'Of course, Miss Bluebell,' I said. 'You won't get any trouble from me.'

But as the week went on it was clear that it wasn't going to work. It just looked strange with me being so much shorter than the other girls.

'This is a complete waste of time,' one of them said during rehearsals. 'I'm six foot in my heels – Irene's way shorter than the rest of us.'

I just stood there feeling like a right Charlie.

I hated every minute of being there. It was freezing cold, and although it was very beautiful we were in the middle of nowhere and I felt trapped.

'It's a bit different to London, eh?' said Audrey.

'I love London,' I sighed.

I was a city girl at heart and I was used to crowds of people, to jumping on Tubes, trains and buses, and heading into the hustle and bustle of the West End. This was a tiny, isolated alpine town at the top of a mountain. I missed the dusty Victorian theatres with their grotty, cramped dressing-rooms and antiquated toilets. There was nothing much in Garmisch except the American army base, and the GIs were constantly chatting up the Bluebells. They were so confident and direct, and they would just come up and start talking to you like they'd known you for years.

'Well, hello there, pretty lady,' one of them said to me. 'I haven't seen you before.'

'That's because I've just got here,' I said.

'Ask the other girls but we can get you anything you want,' he said, flashing me a perfect smile. 'Tights, cigarettes, chewing gum. You name it, we can get it for you, darling. Just give me the word.'

'No, thank you,' I said. 'But that's very kind of you.'

They had the gift of the gab, I'll certainly

give them that, and admittedly they did look handsome in their flash uniforms. Unlike the English soldiers, they all had money too, but I wasn't in awe of them the way the rest of the girls seemed to be. Like a lot of men in those days, they seemed to assume that if you were a dancer you were easy, and treated you like a piece of meat.

But the other Bluebells seemed to dote on the GIs. One of the girls called Pamela came running into the dressing-room one afternoon with a soppy grin plastered across her face.

'Look, girls,' she said. 'Hank got me those nylons he promised and some chewing gum too.'

'Amazing,' said Gertie. 'He promised he'd get me some tins of peaches.'

I couldn't believe how much these girls fawned over the American soldiers and their endless gifts.

'Irene, you should go out with one of them one night,' she told me. 'They know how to show a girl a good time and they're very well-mannered.'

'No, thank you,' I said. 'I'm just not interested.'

I was slightly intimidated by it all and I felt the others were looking down on me because I wasn't falling at the Americans' feet like them.

A lot of English girls fell in love with

Americans during the Second World War. They seemed so glamorous and exciting, but really it was just an illusion. After the war these GI brides, as they were known, went back to the US with them and found themselves living in some remote town in the middle of nowhere.

But one thing about the Americans was that they were persistent, and eventually I caved in and agreed to go out with them one night. There was a group of us going, including Audrey and a couple of the other dancers.

'A few of us boys will take you gals up into the mountains,' said one GI called Fred. 'It's incredible up there at night.'

'OK then,' I said. 'But no funny business.'

The next evening they drove us in their jeeps up to the mountain slopes. It was a clear, crisp night and it was beautiful up there.

'It's so clear you can see all the stars,' I said.

'Not like London, eh, Irene?' laughed Audrey.

Some baby deer had come down from the mountains, and when they saw the lights on the jeeps they were transfixed. They just stood there, absolutely mesmerised, and you could see their eyes glowing a gold colour in the darkness.

'Aren't they lovely?' I said.

I was puzzled when the boys got some shotguns out of the Jeeps.

'What are you doing with those?' I asked Fred.

'Oh, we're just going to have a bit of fun,' he told me.

I was horrified when they started taking pot shots at the baby deer.

'Did you see that one?' laughed one of the GIs. 'Talk about a sitting target.'

I couldn't believe that they were killing baby animals just for fun and laughing about it.

'I can't stay here and watch this. It's cruel,' I said. 'Please can you drive me back?'

I was so upset and I thought it was awful. It certainly wasn't my idea of entertainment and it didn't impress me in the slightest.

After a week of rehearsals it was time for our first show. I was dreading it as I still felt that I looked like the odd one out, being so much shorter than the others. Our costumes were very glamorous and beautifully made, but skimpy. We had to wear a satin bra and knickers so our midriffs were bare, a big fluffy feather headdress, more feathers stuck to our bottoms and the highest heels that I'd ever worn in my life. If they were game, some of the girls went topless, with just a few jewels and feathers to cover their modesty.

Even though it was a prefab, the nightclub was very tastefully decorated inside. There was a small dance floor surrounded by round tables with crisp white tablecloths and dim lighting.

'Blimey,' I said. 'I can't believe how close we are to the audience.'

Performing on the same level as the audience you felt as if you were right next to them. The American soldiers took their seats and soon the place was packed. When the band started we came out to a rapturous reception as the GIs clapped, cheered, slapped their thighs and wolf-whistled. The routine went well but I hated every minute of it. While we danced, the soldiers were eating, drinking and yapping away. Tripping around with hardly anything on was all right if you were on stage in a theatre, but here we were practically right on top of them. I could see the expressions on all their faces, the beer they were drinking and the German sausages on their plates. It wasn't like being in a theatre where the audience's attention is all on you. They were either ignoring us while they smoked, drank and ate their dinner, or they were watching us because we had good figures and nice legs. It seemed alien to me and I felt uncomfortable. What I liked was the skill and discipline of dancing.

'I didn't enjoy it,' I told Audrey as we filed out. 'It didn't feel like dancing to me. I just felt like we were there to be a bit of eye candy.'

'I'm sorry,' she told me. 'I feel awful for persuading you to come all the way out here.'

It was a relief when Miss Bluebell turned up the next day and agreed that I was just too short to work in that troupe.

'You're a good dancer, Miss Starr, and I don't want to lose you,' she said. 'So I'd like to send you to my troupe in Berlin. There's a new nightclub opening and my girls there are much shorter. We can send you on the train today.'

'No, thank you,' I said. 'I don't think cabaret is for me. I just want to go home.'

I'd had enough and I couldn't wait to leave, but I could see Miss Bluebell was annoyed that I was saying no to her.

'It's a great opportunity,' she said. 'And we've already paid your travel expenses out here.'

'I'm really not interested,' I said. 'I'm sorry.'

'Fair enough, then,' she told me. 'Mr Bluebell has some business to attend to in Paris, so he can accompany you there.'

Poor Audrey was upset to see me go.

'I'm sorry for wasting your time, Irene,' she told me. 'But I think you're making a big mistake by not going to Berlin.'

'I want to go back to London,' I said.

I was dreading the long journey home and, if truth were told, I didn't feel entirely comfortable being alone with Mr Bluebell. There was just something about him that I didn't like, but I simply wanted to get home.

The journey was every bit as horrendous as I'd feared. The train that was going to take us across Germany was a horrible, dirty, rickety thing and we were packed in like sardines. There was no food on board so I didn't have anything to eat. I was cold and uncomfortable, and although Mr Bluebell was snoring away next to me most of the way I didn't sleep a wink.

Suddenly in the middle of the night the train came to a violent, shuddering stop. We were in a station at a place called Aachen and suddenly all these officers came storming on board. They had swastikas on their uniforms and were carrying guns as they marched down the aisles. It was dark and cold, and I was absolutely terrified out of my wits. It was one of the only times in my career I can truly say that I felt frightened. I didn't speak German so I didn't know what they wanted.

'Passport,' one of them barked at me.

I showed him my passport with trembling hands and I was so relieved when eventually the train started moving again.

By the time we got to Paris we'd been travelling for thirty-six hours. I still hadn't slept, I hadn't eaten anything, and at times I'd been too frightened to even go to the toilet. All I'd had were a couple of sips of black coffee that tasted like tar.

'Right then, Miss Starr, I'll have to leave you here,' said Mr Bluebell.

I was both relieved and terrified to say goodbye to him. I didn't speak French and I didn't have a clue where I was going, but I eventually found my way to the ferry port. It was the longest, roughest crossing, and I was as sick as a dog. Then finally I caught the coach back to London.

As I staggered through the door, a bedraggled, starving, exhausted mess, I'd never been so grateful to be home. My grandmother was in the front room sewing.

'Oh, what are you doing here?' she said, looking up briefly. 'I thought you were supposed to be in Germany.'

That was that and she went back to her needlework.

I was so relieved to be home. My first trip abroad had certainly been an experience and it had shown me that my real love was theatre. I was back to looking for a job and I was determined never to work in cabaret again.

I'd been back from Germany for a fortnight when Raymond came round one afternoon after he'd finished teaching. He still popped in from time to time and we were playing a game of gin rummy when I realised something strange was going on.

'Raymond, I know this sounds odd, but I can't see out of my left eye,' I told him.

I couldn't see the symbols or read the numbers on any of the playing cards.

'That doesn't sound right, Rene,' he said. 'I'd better get Mother.'

'What do you mean, you can't see?' she said.

'My vision's gone all blurry and I can't see anything out of my left eye,' I explained.

Mum was worried too, so she booked me an emergency appointment with the doctor.

'I'll take you straight down there,' she said.

The doctor examined me.

'Have you banged your eye recently, or has it been giving you any problems?' he asked.

'No,' I said. 'All I know is that I can't see out of it.'

'Hmmm,' he said, examining me. 'I can't tell what's wrong but there's clearly something, so I'm going to send you to Moorfields Eye Hospital.'

I was getting quite frightened by then as my vision was still blurry. I was also terrified of going to hospital, remembering how scared I was when I'd been treated for my ear as a young girl. The specialist looked into my eye and wrote something down on his pad.

'Well?' I said. 'What is it?'

'You've got a detached retina,' he said. 'It's serious but treatable. If we want to save your sight then we've got to move quickly, so I'd like to operate as soon as we can.'

'Operate?' I said, unable to disguise the fear in my voice. 'Is there any other way?'

'I'm afraid not, my dear,' he said.

I knew it had to be done, but I was absolutely terrified. He explained that they could do the operation while I was awake or they could put me completely under. I couldn't bear the thought of somebody cutting into my eye while I watched.

'Please knock me out,' I begged.

There was no time to be scared. A few hours later I said a quick goodbye to Mum as I was wheeled down to theatre. I came round several hours later to what sounded like someone shouting in the bed next to me.

'Nurse, nurse, come 'ere. Me bleedin' boat race is achin'.'

It was a girl's voice and she was shouting about her face hurting, turning the ward blue with her effing and jeffing. I was still groggy from the operation and my left eye was all bandaged up, but I turned my head and tried to focus on her with my good eye. She couldn't have been much more than fourteen and had long blonde hair. I could tell that she was very pretty even though she had two big bandages covering both of her eyes.

'Are you all right?' I asked her, even though I knew she couldn't see me.

'Bloody nurses,' she yelled in a strong cockney accent. 'They don't take no bloody notice. I need the lav and I need some pills as me eyes are killin' me.'

'What are you in here for?' I asked.

'It was them Krays,' she said. 'One of them twins punched me so 'ard in the face the quacks are saying I ain't never gonna see again.'

'Oh, that's awful,' I said. 'I'm so sorry.'

'Don't worry,' she told me. 'Those boys are gonna 'ave it comin' to them when my brothers knock seven bells out of 'em.'

I was so shocked I didn't know what to say. When she was asleep that night I asked one of the nurses about her.

'Is it true what she said about being blind?'

The nurse nodded.

'I'm afraid it is,' she said. 'She was beaten up by a young man, and he gave her two black eyes and completely tore both her retinas. She's lost the sight in both of her eyes.'

It was only when I heard about the notorious gangsters called the Krays and their reign of terror in the East End a few years later that I realised that one of them must have been the same teenage boy who had blinded the girl I'd met in hospital.

At the time her story made me feel lucky that my sight had hopefully been saved, but

141

I was still anxious about when I could go back to work.

'When do you think I'll be able to start dancing again?' I asked the specialist when he came round to see me. 'I need to start going to auditions and look for a job.'

He just tutted and shook his head.

'Just be glad that your eye is mended, young lady,' he snapped.

I was so upset that he'd spoken to me so harshly I burst into tears.

'Don't cry, dear, or you'll wet the bandages over your eye,' the nurse told me, panicking.

It was a very memorable stay in hospital as later that week, on Thursday, 20 November 1947, the country celebrated the wedding of Princess Elizabeth to Philip Mountbatten. The nurses brought a wireless onto the ward and gathered around it excitedly to listen to the ceremony that was only happening a few miles away in Westminster Abbey. We could even hear the cheer of the crowds on the street outside the windows.

But I'd had enough of being in hospital by then and my patience was wearing a bit thin.

'Please can you turn it down?' I asked them. 'I'm an anti-royalist and I don't want to listen to that.'

I could see the nurses were all shocked at my admission, and I felt guilty for ruffling their feathers.

At least Raymond would be proud of me, I thought to myself.

A week after my operation I was discharged from hospital, and thankfully I could see out of my eye again. For another fortnight, though, I had to wear a pair of glasses that looked like two black top hats with little holes in the end, so I could only look straight ahead.

As soon as they were off I knew I needed to start looking for a job. I hadn't worked since I came back from my time in Germany with the Bluebells. I was convinced that dancing in a big troupe was not for me, but the biggest opportunity of my life was just around the corner.

8

Trying Out

A couple of weeks after I'd recovered from my operation, I saw an advert in *The Stage* that caught my attention.

THE JOHN TILLER GIRLS
*Girls needed to perform in a new Tiller
troupe at a top West End theatre.
Only well-trained dancers need apply.*

143

After my brief experience with the Bluebells you would have thought I'd have been put off joining another troupe. But the Tillers were possibly the world's longest-running and most famous dance troupe. Founded by John Tiller in 1886, they were known for their thirty-two-and-a-half high kicks a minute and their precise, synchronised routines, and the idea of performing at a top West End theatre was intriguing.

'I know I said I wanted to do more ballet, but I think I'll give it a go,' I told Mum.

'I've heard the Tillers are very accomplished dancers,' she said.

More out of curiosity than anything I decided to go along. The auditions were being held the following week at a rehearsal room in central London. I knew lots of girls would turn up for a plum job like that and, sure enough, when I arrived the large, dark and dusty hall was already packed full of young women, all dressed in their dance tunics and clutching ballet and tap shoes.

There were two spinsters taking the auditions. They took to the stage and clapped their hands, and a hush descended over the excited crowd.

'It's wonderful to see so many of you have turned up today,' said one them in a well-spoken voice. 'My name is Miss Doris and I'm in charge of troupe management, and this is Miss Barbara our choreographer.'

They were probably only in their fifties, but they looked like two old grannies in their tweed skirts and cardigans, pearl necklaces and flat brown lace-up shoes. With their grey set hair and make-up-free faces, there was nothing glamorous or theatrical about them at all.

'We're thrilled to tell you that we're looking for twenty-five girls to form our new top troupe that we hope will be performing in a new variety show at the London Palladium,' said Miss Doris.

There was a collective intake of breath and a few squeals of excitement as nearly a hundred girls' eyes lit up. I'd never been to the London Palladium before, but it was a world-famous theatre and I knew all the top names in showbiz wanted to work there.

There were a lot of girls to see, and I knew this was going to take a while and involve a fair bit of waiting around. First of all Miss Barbara and Miss Doris got us to stand in lines and they walked up and down the rows. There were girls there of all shapes, sizes and types, from blondes to redheads and brunettes.

'Checking out our legs, no doubt to make sure we can do all that high kicking,' whispered the tall blonde girl standing next to me. 'Apparently Hitler liked this type of dancing, you know, because he thought it was very military.'

'Fancy that,' I smiled.

'I'm Jean by the way,' she said.

'I'm Irene,' I told her. 'Pleased to meet you.'

We all stood there patiently while they walked along and inspected each girl from top to toe, noting the length of our legs and our height. Then they carefully divided us up into five groups, with around twenty girls in each. Miss Barbara went round each group with a notebook.

'I need your names and a telephone number for those of you that have one, at home or at a neighbour's. Or your postal address where we can contact you by telegram if not.'

We were lucky enough to have a phone at my grandparents' house, because my mother and Harry needed to be contactable for work, but in 1948 the majority of people didn't.

Then she organised us into what was known in the business as a graduated line. This meant the tallest girls were at either end ranging down to the shortest in the middle, which gave a uniform look from the audience's point of view. Thankfully height didn't seem to be an issue, as it was with the Bluebells, and I was fourth in from the left.

'Now pay attention, girls,' said Miss Barbara. 'I'm going to show you a simple kick and tap routine that we'd like each group to perform for us.'

We only had about fifteen minutes' instruction and practice, which was normal. As a professional dancer you were expected to pick up routines pretty quickly and remember them.

'With John Tiller's girls it's all about discipline and uniformity,' Miss Barbara told us. 'Every movement must be perfect and there must not even be a hair out of place. You have to dance together almost like you are one woman.

'And remember to smile, girls, please.'

'Yes, Miss Barbara,' we replied in unison.

I knew that they were striving for absolute precision and perfection. Even though I danced professionally, the routine was hard work. We had to link arms round each other's backs and ended it by doing thirty high kicks.

'I'm determined to make a good job of this,' I told Jean.

'Me too,' she said. 'I'd love to work at the Palladium.'

We were the last group to go on stage and we waited at the side while all of the others did their routines.

'And the remaining girls, please,' shouted Miss Doris.

Finally it was our turn, and we trotted onto the stage and lined up. In the corner sat a pianist – a man in a suit with a cigarette hanging out of his mouth. We gave him a nod and he started to play.

'Take it away in three, girls,' shouted Miss Barbara. 'One and two and three...'

Off we went. I wasn't nervous; I just gave it my all and remembered to smile. While we danced our hearts out, Miss Barbara and Miss Doris whispered to each other and took notes.

'Thank you, girls,' Miss Barbara said afterwards. 'We'll be in touch.'

I thought it had gone OK and we'd all been in time, but so many girls had auditioned and I didn't want to get my hopes up. To be honest, I hadn't thought about whether I really wanted the job anyway.

The next day the phone rang.

'Miss Irene Starr?' said a voice.

'Yes.'

'This is Miss Doris from the John Tiller Girls,' she said. 'I'm pleased to say that we were very impressed with your audition and we'd like to offer you a place in the new troupe.'

'Oh,' I said, completely stunned.

I was lost for words.

'Well, dear, would you like to take the job or not?' she asked matter-of-factly.

'I really don't know,' I said. 'Could I please have a think about it?'

She sounded slightly annoyed that I was even hesitating.

'All right then, you do that and we'll call

back tomorrow.'

I put the phone down and looked over at Mum.

'Rene, you naughty thing, what the heck are you playing at?' she said. 'You don't say no to the Tiller Girls.'

'Well, I'm just not sure I want to work for a troupe after what happened with the Bluebells,' I said. 'Plus it's a variety show, and I wanted to try and do more ballet.'

'Rene, it's the Palladium,' she said. 'You don't turn down the Palladium.'

I knew Mum was right. All of the big stars from around the world were queuing up to perform there, and I knew most professional dancers would have given their right arm to appear in the top troupe of Tillers on that famous stage.

'I've probably blown my chances now,' I sighed.

But thankfully Miss Doris kept to her word and she called back the following day.

'Well, Miss Starr,' she said wearily. 'Have you made your decision?'

'Yes,' I said. 'I'd like to take the job, please.'

'Very good, dear,' she replied. 'Rehearsals start at 8 a.m. sharp next Monday.'

'I look forward to seeing you then,' I said.

They were being held in the same hall where we'd gone for the auditions and I couldn't wait to get started. They'd chosen twenty-five girls and I could see we were a mix from several of the groups. Everyone looked very excited and we smiled politely at each other. I noticed that Jean, whom I'd chatted to at the audition, had made it through too, and I gave her a little wave.

'The bosses at the Palladium approached us to put together a troupe to perform in their new American stars variety season,' Miss Doris explained. 'Some of the biggest stars in showbiz will be coming to London and you will hopefully be on the bill with them.

'It's not a done deal, though. In a couple of days we have to audition for the Palladium management and show them the troupe that we've put together, and they will decide if you're good enough. They're auditioning several other troupes of girls, but I want Tillers to get the job, of course.'

The pressure was on.

We were handed our new uniforms that we would have to wear to rehearsals and for the audition at the Palladium. They consisted of a tight white shirt with a little black bow tie safety-pinned onto it, black knickers, and little white ankle socks and black shoes.

Miss Barbara wasted no time in putting us through our paces. She led us through the four-minute routine that involved starting in our line, doing sixteen high kicks on the spot, then sixteen kicks moving forward. Then we had to break up and gallop round in an outward-facing circle and then finish back in the line with thirty-two more high kicks. We soon learned not to kick too high, as it was exhausting with so many of them to do.

Our first attempt didn't go well. Miss Barbara raised her hand to the pianist to stop him.

'Girls, that was a shambles,' she said. 'You must kick on exactly the same count and to exactly the same level.'

The perfect height of a Tiller Girl kick was to hip height and not any higher. Everything had to be absolutely precise and exactly the same, even down to the way we linked our arms.

'To keep the line stable when you're dancing you need to loosely put your arms around each other's waists,' she said. 'Girls on the end of the line, stick your elbows out to the side, fingers to the front and thumbs to the back.

'I expect nothing but perfection, ladies,' said Miss Barbara. 'Now heads up and smile.'

After a few hours my feet hurt and my face literally ached from smiling so much. There was so much to remember, and I knew they had very high standards not only in the way we danced but in the way we behaved too.

'It's important you understand that we're very particular about the type of girl that we

151

take on,' Miss Doris told us. 'We need hard-working and well-behaved young ladies, don't we, Miss Barbara?'

'We certainly don't want to risk anyone bringing the Tiller name into disrepute,' said Miss Barbara sternly. 'We want nice, wholesome young women. The girl next door, if you like.'

I got the feeling that we'd been chosen for our appearance and attitude as much as for our dancing ability. As a Tiller Girl I got the impression that it was frowned upon to have a relationship.

'Do any of you have a gentleman friend?' Miss Doris asked us.

I'm sure a lot of girls did secretly, but only one game girl put her hand up.

'What does he do for living, dear?' Miss Doris asked.

'He's a print-press operator,' she said nervously.

'Well, that's a good, solid job,' she said, nodding approvingly. 'We would very much like to meet him.'

We were told that anyone with a boyfriend had to bring them in so that Miss Barbara and Miss Doris could give them the once over and check that they were decent!

'Do you have a boyfriend?' Miss Doris asked me.

'No, I certainly don't,' I said.

'Very good, dear,' she told me. 'Let's try

and keep it that way.'

It was clear Miss Doris and Miss Barbara were going to be keeping quite a motherly eye over us girls. Miss Doris, with her round, smiling face, seemed very warm and approachable. Miss Barbara, on the other hand, was a bit more bristly and stiff. She was quite quiet and I got the impression she was more of a disciplinarian than sweet Miss Doris. Neither of them had ever married and they shared a house together in Putney.

We practised for two long days at the rehearsal rooms and it gave us a chance to get to know each other. All of us were professional dancers, and some had come down from the North and the Midlands like Peggy and Betty. There was a girl called Kay who seemed nice, a short girl called Ruth, as well as Jean, who was very funny and friendly.

After a couple of days it was time for our big audition at the Palladium and we were all nervous.

'I really hope we don't mess it up,' sighed Jean.

'We won't,' I said.

The actual routine was quite simple. The only tricky part was making sure that we were all in time. Every movement had to be perfect – even our heads had to turn simultaneously.

'Now, girls, you need to look immaculate tomorrow,' Miss Doris told us. 'Clean uniforms, lots of make-up and big smiles.'

We'd all arranged to meet outside the theatre first. I'd never set foot in the Palladium before, but even just walking up the marble steps at the front gave me butterflies in my tummy.

'It's very grand, isn't it?' said Peggy.

'Hello, ladies,' said the doorman in his top hat and red jacket, holding the front door open for us.

As soon as I saw the foyer I knew that I really wanted this.

'It's beautiful,' I said as we walked up the grand staircase with its huge mahogany banister and thick red carpet. Inside the auditorium it was even more stunning, with its red and gold décor.

'Wow,' I gasped, taking in the plush red velvet seats, the ornately carved gold boxes and the heavy red curtain that stretched across the enormous stage. The Palladium even had its own telephone system, so people sitting in the boxes could call each other, and a revolving stage that I'd never seen the likes of before.

I'd worked in a lot of theatres by then, but even when the Palladium was empty you could just tell that there was a special atmosphere about it. It wasn't the biggest theatre, with just over two thousand seats, but it seemed so grand. I was completely bowled over by the place.

'You've got fifteen minutes to practise and familiarise yourself with the routine before the audition,' Miss Doris told us.

We all lined up on the enormous stage behind the red velvet curtain and started rehearsing.

'Remember, girls. Eyes, tits and teeth,' joked Jean, and we all fell about laughing.

'Ladies!' said Miss Barbara. 'Less of the chin-wagging, please. Mr Parnell is just about ready to start.'

We were going to be performing our routine for the managing director of Moss Empires, who ran the Palladium – a man called Val Parnell. He was sitting in the front row of the auditorium with Miss Barbara and Miss Doris.

'Whenever you're ready, girls, take it away,' he yelled.

Then it was curtain up and off we went. After we had finished we stood there completely out of breath and looked towards Mr Parnell for his reaction. To our relief and delight he was up on his feet, clapping and grinning from ear to ear.

'Absolutely brilliant, girls,' he boomed. 'You're hired!'

Miss Barbara and Miss Doris were ecstatic, and we were all very excited. He took us straight up to the office to sign our contracts for the first three-month variety season.

'I'll get a stage-hand to give you a tour

round,' he told us. 'If you're going to be Palladium girls you need to know where everything is. You'll soon know every nook and cranny of this place.'

I still couldn't believe we were going to be working there. We trooped after the stage-hand and followed him backstage. Even though the inside of the Palladium was grand and magnificent, the backstage area certainly wasn't.

'These are the stars' dressing-rooms,' he said. 'So the likes of Frank Sinatra and Bob Hope will be getting ready in here.'

'Wow, Frank Sinatra,' whispered one of the girls, who was called Sylvia.

I was surprised by how tiny the rooms were, and there was nothing fancy about them. They were just ordinary rooms with bare walls, a wooden table and chair, and a mirror with light bulbs around it.

'This is the green room, where you can get teas or coffees during rehearsals and where some of the acts wait in between appearing on stage,' he said.

I knew that historically they were painted green, which was how they got their name, but the one at the Palladium wasn't.

'I'll take you to your dressing-room now, girls,' he said.

'Ooh, I can't wait to see it,' whispered Peggy.

We all followed him up three flights of a

very steep stone staircase right to the top of the building, and there, practically underneath the roof, was our new home. It was a fairly big room, but it would be cramped considering there were going to be twenty-five of us getting ready in there.

There was a long mirror surrounded by lights and a table along one side of the room. We each had a chair, and there were a couple of washbasins and a long rail running down the centre for our costumes.

Miss Barbara and Miss Doris came up to see us.

'Very well done, girls,' Miss Doris told us. 'But now the hard work really starts. We've got two weeks to learn the routines for the first show.'

They explained that they already had a troupe of Tiller Girls at the Victoria Palace theatre and one at the Adelphi, so they couldn't be there all the time to watch over us.

'Every troupe has its own head girl who will call rehearsals and keep a watchful eye over everyone,' said Miss Doris. 'We'd like to appoint Kay as your head girl.'

'Well done, Kay,' said Miss Barbara, and we all gave her a round of applause.

Kay was one of the oldest girls and she was one of the smallest too. She had short, dark hair and a neat little figure, and she seemed very nice.

'Kay is a very experienced dancer and it's her job to keep you in line,' said Miss Doris. 'She'll be making sure that you're always on time for rehearsals and don't let the Tiller name down outside the theatre.

'She'll also be writing us a weekly report to let us know about any issues or problems.'

'We'd better keep on her good side, then,' whispered Jean to me.

I knew by then that it was going to be fun but it was also going to be damn hard work, and I couldn't wait to get started.

9

Bright Lights

I stood there in my underwear, as still as a statue, while the woman measured me from top to toe.

'That's lovely, darling,' she said, putting her tape measure around her neck and writing it all down in a notebook. 'This should only take a few more minutes.'

We had come to a top West End theatrical costumier called Morris Angel's to be fitted for our costumes for the new show. Behind me was a long queue of girls all waiting for their turn.

'There will be a costume change for each dance that you do,' Miss Barbara had told us. 'So you'll need four outfits per show.'

As the Palladium Tiller Girls, as we were now known, we would open the show, close the first half, open the second half and close the show, appearing on stage at the end with the Hollywood star. It amounted to a heck of a lot of costumes, and as we were the top troupe they were all going to be brand new and made to measure for each girl.

It was going to be hard work. We had to do two matinees a week on a Wednesday and Thursday, and one show a night at 7.30 p.m. every day except Sunday. Then every two weeks we had to learn a new show for the next American star, which would mean another set of new costumes and dance routines. So for the first twelve-week season we'd need around twenty-four costumes each.

It felt like a real luxury having time off from rehearsals to go to this famous West End costumier. We'd traipsed up the stairs of the old Victorian warehouse in Shaftesbury Avenue, and had to strip off to our bra and knickers and line up to be measured.

For the first season alone we needed cowboy outfits, sailor suits, pirate outfits and pony outfits, as well as an array of beautiful evening dresses that were worth hundreds of pounds each.

'We'll make up the patterns out of brown paper first and then cut out the material by hand,' the seamstress told me. 'All the sequins and the beading will be done by hand too.'

'Oh, I can't wait to see them,' I said to Jean as we got dressed. 'I've never had brand new costumes made especially for me before.'

'Me neither,' she said. 'I'm used to trying to dance in a dress that's way too tight and won't do up at the back, or worrying about slipping on stage in shoes that are two sizes too big for me.'

There was a highly skilled team of dressmakers, seamstresses and pattern cutters on standby waiting to work on the costumes so that they'd be ready in time for opening night.

A week later it felt like Christmas as we arrived at the Palladium one morning for rehearsals to find the rail in our dressing-room filled with our new costumes. They each had a label pinned into them with our names on and they were absolutely beautiful.

'Oh, my goodness,' I said. 'They're simply stunning.'

The bodices were all boned, and they were lined in satin and velvet with large hooks and eyes on the back so they could be whipped on and off easily. My favourite were the evening dresses. They were short so we could high-kick in them and they were

ABOVE: As a child, I loved posing for the camera. I was nine years old here and this was taken just before the Second World War started. Little did I know how life was going to change.

ABOVE: I did three Royal Command performances during my career and they were always very exciting and nerve-racking. I did one while I was at Italia Conti and two with the Tiller Girls at the Palladium. This was my final one in 1952.

ABOVE: This is me doing my bit to cheer up the troops by posing for a pin-up picture that appeared in *Blighty* magazine.

RIGHT: Posing on the stairs at the Grosvenor hotel with Bob Hope and the rest of the Tillers after we'd done our charity concert for injured servicemen.
I was so shocked by how disfigured some of those poor men were.

ABOVE: Doing some high kicks for the German press on the steps of the train station as we arrived in Dortmund.

DIE ORIGINAL TILLER GIRLS

AB 3. NOVEMBER IM VARIETÉ-TEIL

ABOVE: Our tour of West Germany made history as we were the first English dance troupe to perform there after the war.

ABOVE: Kaye and me on our wedding day in March 1952 outside my grandparents' house in Battersea. I was back at work at the Palladium the next day.

ABOVE: Mum came up to Scarborough to see me while I was doing a summer season there with the Tillers. It was the first and only time she ever saw me dance.

LEFT: A publicity shot from when I performed in *Aladdin* at the London Casino and got a shock when I saw Orson Welles in the front row of the audience.

designed to show off our long legs. One was a very vivid pink colour with a black lace trim, and another was made out of beautiful blue silk taffeta with a boned bodice and puff sleeves. As well as the costumes there were headdresses, hats and gloves to match.

'They're so glamorous and pretty,' I sighed.

I couldn't wait to wear them.

Rehearsals were now in full swing as the first performer – the American actor and comedian Danny Kaye – was due to open the new variety season on Monday, 2 February 1948.

Every day Miss Barbara would put us through our paces. She had swapped her tweed skirt for a pair of sensible trousers as she taught us the routines.

'Let's start in the line with sixteen kicks,' she shouted. 'Off you go, jump kick, jump kick. Smile, girls, show those teeth. Come on, kick those legs, ladies.'

There was no doubt about it, it was damn hard work.

We also had a ballet number to learn, which we did on pointe shoes, and a dance that involved us waving around giant pink feather fans that were bigger than us.

'Into a circle, please, and waft them around,' said Miss Barbara.

It had been drummed into us by then that it all had to be seamless and there was no room for mistakes.

'For the first week of shows Miss Doris and I will be in the audience every night just to make sure that it's all perfect,' she said. 'If it isn't, then Kay will be calling extra rehearsals. Every night of the season, even if we're not there, there will be someone in the audience checking that everything is faultless.'

We all wanted to avoid extra rehearsals if we could, as we knew it would be exhausting to rehearse all day as well as perform at night.

'You need to give 110 per cent to every performance,' Miss Doris told us. 'You may have done the same routine hundreds of times, but you need to give the same energy and commitment that you did to it the first time. It will be the first time most people in the audience will have seen the show; they don't know that you're tired or you've done a matinée as well that day.'

We only had two weeks to perfect our routine. We'd start at 9 a.m. and rehearse all day. At midday we'd break for lunch and all dash across the road from the theatre to a little café on Carnaby Street. I always had the same thing – mushroom stalks on toast. I'd never had mushrooms before, so I thought they were really exotic, and it was one of the cheapest things on the menu.

'You're going to turn into a mushroom if you're not careful,' warned Sylvia.

We were always served by the same

plump, middle-aged waiter, who was very camp. As soon as we all trooped in wearing our uniforms his eyes lit up. When we told him that we were Tiller Girls he looked like he was going to pass out with excitement.

'Dancing girls!' he cried. 'What an honour to serve you ladies.'

He always made such a fuss of us and wanted to know how rehearsals were going.

'Is that handsome fellow Frank Sinatra there yet?' he asked.

'He's not on for a couple of weeks,' I told him.

'Well,' he said, lowering his voice. 'Make sure you put in a good word for me.'

'I think his lady friend Ava Gardner might have something to say about that,' I joked.

Our music was going to be provided by a band called the Skyrockets. Instead of hiring an orchestra, as was normal in a West End theatre, Val Parnell had taken a chance and hired a dance band for the first time.

'Say hello to the Tiller Girls,' Mr Parnell said as he introduced us to the musicians.

The band were a bunch of older, grey-haired men who'd been together for years, having all met while they were in the RAF.

We were also introduced to the stage manager Jack Matthews, who seemed lovely. He was one of those people who pretended to be grumpy and grumbled all the time but he loved it really.

163

The Sunday before the opening of the season on the Monday, all of the cast and crew had a full dress and technical rehearsal. It was a chance for everyone to run through their acts, to test the lights and make sure they were positioned in the best spot.

I was so excited as we all got changed into the beautiful blue taffeta silk ball dresses that we were going to wear for our opening number. Mine fitted like a glove.

Miss Barbara and Miss Doris were watching as we ran through our routine on stage.

'Well done, girls,' said Miss Barbara. 'That was perfect. Do that on Monday and management will be very happy.'

'Why don't you all go for a break in the green room and grab a drink while they sort out the lights?' said Miss Doris. 'It's going to be a while before your next number.'

We headed to the green room and queued up with all the other cast and crew for tea and coffee.

'There's Danny Kaye,' whispered Anne, pointing to the redheaded man with a rather large nose queuing up in front of me.

He looked like an ordinary bloke to me, but it was very exciting to think I was inches away from a Hollywood star. I was busy staring at him but he obviously hadn't seen me behind him in the queue. When he turned around he bumped straight into me and spilt boiling hot coffee all down me and the front of my brand new, hugely expensive silk dress. I yelped in pain and all the other girls gasped. Danny Kaye didn't say a word and just wandered off.

'Oh, my God,' I said, panicking. 'What am I going to do? Miss Barbara's going to kill me.'

My dress, which I knew had cost an absolute fortune, was completely ruined and I was so worried I was going to get an almighty rollicking.

'Go and see Rosie,' said Kay. 'She won't be very happy but she'll be able to sort it out.'

Rosie was the Palladium's in-house wardrobe mistress who was in charge of any day-to-day repairs that we needed doing. She was a very plump, jolly woman with a heaving bosom. Her face fell when I showed her the big brown stain down the front of my beautiful dress, and I thought she was going to burst into tears.

'It wasn't my fault,' I blurted. 'Please don't shout at me. Danny Kaye did it.'

I knew she couldn't get cross at the Hollywood star who was topping the bill.

'Dearie me,' she said, shaking her head as she inspected the damage. 'You can't clean this delicate type of material, so I'm going to have to cut this stained panel out completely and replace it.'

I felt terribly guilty, as she was going to have to take it home with her to fix so it would be ready in time for tomorrow's show.

'Thank you,' I said. 'I'm so grateful.'

Soon it was time for opening night. I arrived an hour and a half before the show to give myself plenty of time to get ready, and our dressing-room was already a hive of activity. There were girls running around in their underwear, doing their make-up or nipping up onto the roof to have a cigarette as we weren't allowed to smoke in the dressing-room.

'Hi, Irene,' said Jean. 'I've got the jitters, I can't sit still. How are you feeling?'

'I'm way more excited than nervous,' I told her. 'I'd better hurry up and put some slap on.'

I couldn't wait to get on that famous stage and perform. Like with any show, we were responsible for buying and applying our own stage make-up, which we kept in a wooden box. I stripped down to my blue satin bra and cotton pants, tied a scarf around my head and got to work.

I'd been taught how to do stage make-up at Italia Conti, and every girl did exactly the same. First of all I got out my Leichner grease paint. These were greasy pan sticks that came in three shades. I put a very pale one on first, which I dotted all over my face and blended in, followed by a medium shade and then finally a darker one. You kept applying and blending them until you'd

166

got the right colour for your face. It looked quite thick and orangey, as if you'd got bad sunburn, but under the stage lights it made your face stand out.

'Who's got my carmine?' I yelled.

This was a bright red pigment powder that we rubbed into our cheeks to give us a bit of colour.

'Sorry, Irene,' said Peggy. 'I'm just borrowing a bit.'

Next I put blue cream eye shadow on my lids and carefully lined my eyes with black kohl eyeliner on the top and the bottom and flicked it out. In between where the two lines ended at the outside corner of my eye I drew a horizontal white stripe. Then I put a red dot on the inside corner of my eyes either side of my nose. Everyone in the theatre did this little trick as it was supposed to make your eyes look bigger when you were on stage. There was no such thing as mascara or false eyelashes in the Forties, so to draw attention to our eyes under the bright stage lights we used something called hot black.

'Has anyone got a candle that I can borrow?' I asked above the din.

'Here you go,' said Sylvia, pushing one over to my part of the bench.

I got out a stick of black grease paint, chopped a bit off the end and put it on a spoon, which I then held over the lit candle. When the grease had melted, I got a matchstick and dipped the end in the black stuff, let it cool for a second and then blobbed a bit onto the end of each eyelash. Then I finished off with lots and lots of bright red lipstick.

'I think I'm done,' I said, admiring my handiwork in the mirror.

'Don't forget to put on your wet white,' yelled Kay. 'Otherwise it won't be dry.'

'I hope they've gone easy on the meths in this bottle, otherwise it will sting to high heaven,' said Jean.

Stockings were very expensive and still scarce in those days, and instead we all put this stuff called wet white on our legs so they would all look the same colour. It was a mix of zinc oxide, glycerine, rosewater and methylated spirits that turned an orangey brown colour and looked a bit like fake tan does today. It used to be the head girl's job to make it up every night before a show, but it was always so messy and by now thankfully you could buy pre-mixed glass bottles of it from a theatrical make-up shop. There was a certain knack to applying it that I'd perfected over the years since I'd been working as a professional dancer. I'd pour some into my hands, spit into it as that made it stick better, rub my hands together then smear it over my legs. It was always freezing cold, especially when you were putting it on in winter, and it took ages to dry.

You always had to remember to wash your wet white off at the end of a show. Once when I was working on a panto while I was at Italia Conti, I'd not washed the wet white off well enough or dried my legs properly before going home in the freezing cold. By the end of the week my poor legs were getting terribly chapped and sore, and then I had to put wet white over the top, which made them sting even more. It was agony, so I made sure I never made the same mistake again.

It was pandemonium in the dressing-room as everyone got into their costumes.

'Who's got my shoes?' screeched Peggy.

'They're under your chair,' yelled Jean.

'Will someone help me pin this flower into my hair?' I asked.

I had about fifty Kirby grips, as there was no way I wanted to risk it falling out while we were dancing.

Just then the call boy came running up the steep flight of stairs into our dressing-room.

'Five minutes, girls,' he yelled.

'Do you mind?' joked Kay. 'We're practically in the altogether up here.'

'Don't worry, ladies,' he grinned. 'I've seen it all before.'

He didn't bat an eyelid at the sight of twenty-five girls running around in various states of undress.

'You cheeky little imp,' laughed Peggy.

All of us girls loved teasing the call boy. He was a little blond lad who couldn't have been any more than fifteen. His job was to go around the whole theatre telling everyone how long it was until curtain up. He'd give us a shout an hour before, half an hour before, 'a quarter hour' before and then the five-minute call. His very final call was for 'overture and beginners', which meant the orchestra was preparing to start. Beginners were the very first performers due on stage, which always meant us. If we heard that call and we were still in our dressing-room, then we knew that we'd had it and we'd have to tear down the steps like raving lunatics. It happened sometimes if one of the girls was in the toilet. Even though Jack the stage manager wouldn't be best pleased, he would always hold the curtain for you.

'Come on, ladies,' said Kay. 'It's time.'

On that first night we all trooped down the winding stone stairs in our Cuban-heeled black shoes and waited in the wings for the nod to assume our positions on stage. You could practically feel the nerves and excitement in the air. Everyone was tense because it was the opening night of a new season and this was the first time big Hollywood stars had been invited over to perform in an English variety theatre. The management was worried that it would be a big flop, so there was a lot riding on this opening night. But as soon as the tickets had gone on sale they'd sold out, and we knew we'd be performing to a full house every night. People were excited to think that they were seeing in the flesh stars that they'd only ever seen before in films. We knew this first show had to be a success, or there was a chance it could be canned and we'd all be out of a job.

'Take your positions please, girls,' said Jack.

We all lined up at the back of the stage facing the audience and linked our arms around each other's backs.

'Good luck, girls,' whispered Kay. 'Let's make sure it's perfect.

'And don't forget to smile.'

I ran through the routine in my head. I knew every single kick and step had to be flawless, especially as Miss Doris and Miss Barbara were sitting out there with the Palladium management watching us like hawks.

I saw to the right of me that Jack was on his intercom to the Skyrockets in the pits.

'Take it away,' I heard him say to their musical director Woolf Phillips.

My heart was pounding as loudly as the drum roll that followed, and I felt a shiver of nerves and excitement rush through me. But there was no time to panic as seconds later the Skyrockets launched straight into an up-tempo, high-octane big-band number. The noise was deafening as the twenty-four musicians started to play their instruments and we kicked off.

As the red velvet curtain slowly began to rise I was hit by an overwhelming mix of lights, sound and colour. I'd never experienced anything like it before in my life and it took my breath away. It was almost like being on a different planet. The power of the music pulsed through me – the trumpets and trombones blared out and the cymbals crashed, all in contrast to the tuneful melodies of the clarinets and the other woodwind instruments. The lights were dazzling and I could feel their intense heat on my skin. They were so bright and powerful I could hardly see anything, but I could make out the deep red of the thick velvet curtain and the ornate gold of the boxes to the side of the stage glinting in the spotlights. I couldn't see anyone and the whole auditorium looked black, but I could hear the loud applause of the two-thousand-strong audience as we high-kicked our way to the front of the stage.

The adrenalin surged through my body as I danced as if my life depended on it, turning my head in perfect time with Sylvia, who was one side of me, and Dorothy on the other. I didn't need to mentally remember the steps; it was instinctive and I was carried along by the rhythm of the music. As I danced all I felt was pure, unadulterated joy.

It didn't matter that my Tube journey had been slow that day, that I'd got a spot on my nose or that Harry had been getting on my nerves at home. As soon as I stepped onto that famous stage everything else was forgotten in an instant. For the short time I was up there nothing mattered except the music and the dancing.

I didn't need to remember to smile, I was grinning naturally as I was enjoying every exhilarating minute of it. That's when it finally hit me. I was a dancer. This was what I was born to do, and all I'd ever wanted to do was perform.

Three minutes later and it was all over as our long line high-kicked its way off to stage left.

The audience's applause was still ringing in my ears and I felt like my chest was going to explode, as I'd held my breath for most of the routine.

'Off you go, girls,' shouted Jack. 'Out of the way, please. No hanging around.'

We weren't allowed to linger at the side of the stage to watch the next act. It was very cramped back there, so there was always a mad rush to clear the wings for the next performer. We also needed to get back quickly to change our costumes. As fast as we could, we ran up three flights of stairs back to our dressing-room.

'That was amazing,' gasped Peggy.

'Did you hear the roar of the crowd?' said Jean.

'What an incredible buzz,' I sighed.

I was on a high. Being on stage had given me a huge adrenalin rush, and now I'd experienced it I wanted to do it all over again. But there was no time to sit around congratulating ourselves. We had to get ready for our next number. Danny Kaye wasn't due on until the second half, before which there were a number of variety acts such as singers, comedians and acrobats. The rest of the show whizzed by and thankfully it seemed to go down well. When we came offstage after opening the second half, I could see Danny Kaye waiting in the wings.

'He looks absolutely terrified,' whispered Peggy.

He was really nervous and panicking so much about what the audience's reaction would be that Jack literally had to push him on stage. But he went down a storm, and right up in our dressing-room we could hear the crowd roaring with laughter as he performed the famous Cab Calloway number 'Minnie the Moocher'.

During the show we heard that he invited a little girl from the audience to come up on stage and sing with him. Afterwards he invited her and her parents back to his dressing-room, where he gave them their first taste of Coke.

'He seems like a nice, kind man,' I said to one of the stage-hands, but he shook his head.

'He's a nightmare to work with and his wife's an absolute dragon,' he moaned.

The show finished just after 10 p.m. and we raced up the stairs and all rushed for the sinks to wash our wet white off. We had big tin pots of greasy paraffin that we used to take our make-up off along with some old rags that we'd all brought in from home. We'd leave our dirty rags piled up on the table, and a lady came in every evening and collected them so they were washed and ready for the following day's show.

By the time I'd taken off my make-up, washed off my wet white and hung my costumes up, I always seemed to be the last to leave. Some of the other girls would meet their boyfriends after the show, so they'd always dash off, but I had nothing in particular to rush back for and I liked to leave everything neat and tidy on my bench for the following day. I knew George the doorman quite well by now after two weeks of rehearsals. He had a little office that was more like a cupboard by the stage door so he could check who was coming in and out.

'Last one out as usual, Irene,' he said with a wink.

'See you tomorrow, George,' I smiled.

Then I dashed to the Tube at Oxford

Circus to make sure that I caught the last train home to Clapham. Seeing me in my ordinary winter clothes and with my face free of make-up, you'd never have guessed that less than an hour earlier I'd been dancing around the stage of the world's most famous theatre with a big Hollywood star.

All the glamour and glitz had been left behind at the theatre door but I was still buzzing from our first performance. As I caught the Tube home I smiled to myself. I knew by then I was going to love every second of being a Palladium Tiller Girl.

10

Sisterhood

As the first few weeks of the show went by we soon got into the swing of things. We were working in such close proximity to each other every day that the twenty-five of us soon developed a sisterly bond. We spent a lot of time in our dressing-room between routines, and we'd gossip and chat about all sorts of things – boys, the show, knickers.

'What are we going to do about our pants, girls?' Kay asked one day.

Many of our costumes consisted of a

bodice top with a tight pair of knickers and you would wear your own pants underneath. But there was no such thing as high-cut briefs in those days.

'It looks awful if you can see our undies poking out underneath our costumes,' said Peggy.

'Why don't we knit some, then?' said Sylvia.

She was an avid knitter and she brought in some thick embroidery cotton and patiently showed us all how to cast off. We all bought or borrowed knitting needles and from then on, whenever we had a spare moment, we'd sit there in our dressing-room like a group of old grannies knitting countless pairs of high-cut cotton knickers.

'Who says showbiz isn't glamorous?' joked Jean.

But we really did need lots of spare knickers, especially when it was the time of the month, which was always a nightmare for us girls. Sanitary towels were so big and bulky in those days, and you had to keep them in place by wearing an elasticated sanitary belt around your waist, which was very tricky when you were doing energetic dance routines in tight, skimpy costumes. Some of us would wear four or five pairs of knickers underneath our outfits to avoid any embarrassing leaks.

'It's the wrong time of the month,' I'd say

to the others.

A lot of the girls had the same problem and we'd all look out for each other.

Even though we were all professionally trained dancers none of our troupe had ever worked at the Palladium before. We were all under the same pressure to make sure it was perfect so we'd help each other out with any problems. Several of the girls weren't from London and were living away from home for the first time. There were girls as young as seventeen or eighteen like me; others were in their early twenties like Kay, the head girl. Some of the younger girls were struggling as they were terribly homesick. Many of them had been put up in the Theatre Girls Club in Greek Street, Soho, which provided cheap accommodation for young girls working in the London theatres, but they weren't very happy there.

'We all have to share a room, there's never enough water and we can't unpack our cases because there's no wardrobe,' said Anne.

'It was so cold the other night we all had to get into bed with each other,' said Sylvia.

Ruth just burst into tears.

'I miss my mum and dad,' she sobbed. 'I've never been away from them for this long before.'

She was such a sweet girl and I hated seeing her upset like that.

'You'll be OK,' I said. 'You'll soon get used to it.'

I was so accustomed to being on my own away from my family that it had become second nature to me, but I understood how they felt.

'Well, I feel sorry for you girls having to stay there,' I told them. 'It sounds really dreary and depressing.'

'The one good thing is that it only costs thirty shillings a week to stay there, so at least we've got some of our wages left to send home,' said Sylvia.

It made me feel really lucky that I could work at the Palladium and still live at home. I was used to London and knew it like the back of my hand, so it wasn't a big culture shock for me.

As the weather got warmer, our dressing-room at the top of the theatre got unbearably hot.

'Let's go outside,' said Jean. 'It's so stuffy in here.'

So we all climbed up the small staircase and went out onto the flat roof that over-looked Regent Street and Oxford Street.

We all sat there in our bra and knickers on the boiling hot tarmac, chatting and watching the traffic.

'Anyone want a cigarette?' said Ruth, lighting up.

'No, thanks,' I told her.

Most of us smoked, but I only ever had one a day. Like my mother I smoked a brand called De Reszke Minors, which came in a little red box.

'I hope no one can see us all out here in our underwear,' laughed Jean.

The conversation soon moved on to politics, which would probably have been a shock to all those people who assumed we must be airheads.

'A lot of people think that because you're a dancer, you're silly,' I said. 'I know my aunts do. They're surprised when you have an opinion about things.'

One of the girls, Betty, who was from Yorkshire, was very left-wing like me. Her full name was Betty Boothroyd and years later she became the first woman Speaker of the House of Commons. Proof indeed that you could be a Tiller Girl and have brains! She only did one season with us before she left.

Anne and I would always have heated discussions, as she was quite right-wing. But it was harmless fun. We all had to get along: working together six days a week in such a confined space meant we couldn't afford to fall out. And if we did we knew Kay would have to put it in her weekly report to Miss Doris and Miss Barbara, and they wouldn't be happy about it. In the Tiller Girls you all had to toe the line.

One thing we didn't tell Miss Barbara and Miss Doris about was the séance that we held in the dressing-room.

'Have you lot heard about the ghost?' Jean said one evening while we were putting on our make-up before the show.

'What do you mean?' said Peggy, her face falling. 'What ghost?'

'Oh, don't listen to her,' I smiled. 'Every theatre is supposed to be haunted. Why do you think they all have a ghost light?'

A ghost light was a little light on the stage that was always left on. It came from an old theatrical legend that said if the auditorium ever went completely dark then the ghosts would get lonely and realise everyone had gone home and cause all sorts of mischief.

'No, it's definitely true,' said Jean. 'The stage-hands told me the Palladium has a resident ghost. She glides up and down the crimson staircase at the back of the royal circle in a yellow crinoline dress.'

We all sat there as Jean described how people believed it was the ghost of Helen Campbell.

'She was a former resident of Argyll House, which was the building that stood on the site of the Palladium before it became a theatre,' she said.

By the time she had finished her story, we were all scared out of our wits.

'I know,' said Anne. 'After the show tonight why don't we hold a séance and see if we can contact her?'

'Yes!' said Peggy. 'I'm game.'

I wasn't convinced, so I asked Eric, one of the stage-hands.

'Is this theatre haunted?' I said.

'Oh, most definitely,' he replied. 'You don't want to stay here past eleven o'clock. All sorts of strange things might happen.'

'I bet he's only saying that because he wants to go home,' whispered Peggy.

The stage-hands were in charge of clearing up and they were normally the last ones to leave the theatre. But by then we'd whipped ourselves up into a frenzy, and that night after the show had finished we all sat around a big table in our dressing-room. We put a glass in the centre and placed our hands on it.

'Is there anybody there?' asked Jean.

We were already terrified. Most of the staff had gone home and the theatre was dark, dusty and eerily quiet.

'It's so cold in here,' I whispered, shivering.

'Is there anybody there?' asked Jean again. 'Speak to us.'

I don't know whether it was the pressure of all our fingers pressing on it or just the power of our imaginations, but suddenly the glass seemed to twitch slightly.

We were all terrified and no one dared move.

'Helen Campbell?' whispered Jean. 'Is that you?'

Suddenly the glass shot across the table. We all screamed and jumped out of our skins.

'Did you see that?' yelled Sylvia. 'It moved. There's someone here!'

'Well, I'm not staying to find out who it is,' I said.

I'd never seen us all move so fast. We grabbed our things and hurried out of the dressing-room as fast as we could, and we never mentioned it again.

Miss Barbara came into the dressing-room to see us the next morning.

'I've got some good news, girls,' she said. 'Moss Empires have bought you all some stockings to wear.'

We were delighted as that meant one thing – no more wet white. The stockings were the same 'American tan' colour and they were made from very thick, heavy cotton. Nylon tights weren't invented until a few years later and until then everyone wore stockings.

'Kay will show you how to keep them up,' Miss Barbara told us.

'It's a little bit complicated and you'll need a couple of pennies,' she said.

We all watched as she showed us what to do. First we had to tie a piece of elastic around our waists, then we had to tuck the top of the stockings around an old-fash-

183

ioned penny – much bigger than today's equivalent. Then we got some tape, wrapped it around the penny and looped it over the elastic belt around our waists.

'What a palaver,' I sighed. 'It's going to take ages to get the hang of this.'

But it would be so nice to finish the show and not have to worry about getting to the sinks to wash the wet white off before we went home.

That afternoon we had a matinée performance and we couldn't wait to wear our new stockings. But halfway through the opening number I was dancing away with a big smile on my face when I suddenly felt a ping.

Oh, Lord, I thought to myself.

I knew exactly what was happening. My new stockings had come loose from the elastic around my waist and they were falling down. As I high-kicked away, I felt them sliding slowly down my legs. I couldn't stop or say anything as I had to carry on dancing, but I must have looked a right Charlie. There I was, supposed to be a glamorous Tiller Girl, and instead I had wrinkly stockings around my ankles like Nora Batty!

'My stockings came down,' I wailed, as soon as I was safely at the side of the stage. 'I hope the audience couldn't see them.'

Of course, the Skyrockets in the orchestra pit had noticed and they were all in hysterics.

'Oh, poor Irene,' said Pat the piano player. 'We saw your stockings come down when you were dancing.'

'I hope your drawers are a bit more secure,' laughed the trumpet player.

'You rotten buggers,' I said, completely mortified.

'Oh, what is the management going to say?' I said. I was so worried that I was going to get a telling off. But to my relief, Miss Barbara and Miss Doris were very apologetic.

'Don't worry, girls, we won't make you wear them again,' Miss Doris told us. 'They're obviously not secure enough for you to dance in. We'll go and tell the Palladium bosses that it's impossible to keep them up.'

'Thank you, Miss Doris,' I said. 'I'm ever so sorry about what happened.'

They seemed more annoyed with the band for laughing at me.

The Skyrockets were the jokers in the theatre and they were always teasing us girls or playing tricks on us whenever they could. They all liked a drink, and in the interval some of them would rush out of the theatre and into the Argyll Arms pub opposite, where they would quickly down an ale or two. A few of them would be quite tiddly by the end of the day.

'Did you know, girls, that the pub was named after the 2nd Duke of Argyll, who used to live in the house that was here before the Palladium was built?' said Arthur, the clarinet player.

'Oh, fascinating, Arthur,' Brenda teased.

'Apparently there used to be a secret tunnel connecting the mansion to the pub,' he said.

'I bet you wish that was still there now, eh, Arthur?' I joked.

As it was, they always made it back in the nick of time to take their places in the pit for the second act.

The worst trick that they played on us was the day they deliberately played our music double time. It was during a matinée performance, and as the music started and we began to dance we knew straight away there was something wrong. It was hard enough to get all the kicks into our routine anyway, never mind at double time.

'They're playing our music too fast,' whimpered Kay through gritted teeth.

Our legs must have just looked like a blur as we tried desperately to keep up. We were so cross, but we couldn't let the audience see there was anything amiss – we had to keep dancing away with a big grin plastered on our faces.

But we could see all the Skyrockets laughing at us from the pits and we were furious. And by the time we came offstage we were exhausted as well.

'How could they do that to us?' said Jean.

'I hope they're going to be hauled over the coals by the management for that one.'

'I could bloody kill them,' said Brenda. 'It's lucky we all managed to keep going.'

We didn't speak to them for a whole week we were so annoyed. But whatever happened on or off stage, life at the Palladium was never boring.

11

Dancing with the Stars

Everyone in the dressing-room was in a real tizzy. I'd never seen the girls as excited as this before.

'Frank Sinatra,' sighed Jean. 'I can't believe we're about to work with Frank Sinatra.'

Ol' Blue Eyes himself was heading to the Palladium the following day to start a two-week run and the whole theatre was buzzing. Frank Sinatra was a huge star, a megastar in fact, and this was the first time that he had ever appeared in the UK.

After a few weeks of the new variety season, we were playing to a sell-out audience every night and the stars kept flocking over. Everybody wanted to perform at the Palladium, so Val Parnell had no problem attracting all of the big American names. It was a huge accolade for them to appear at this prestigious theatre too, and they knew that being top of the bill there was the pinnacle of their career. As everyone in the business said – you know you've made it when you've made the Palladium.

British audiences jumped at the chance to see these famous Hollywood film stars in the flesh, and it gave them a big boost after the austerity of the war years. We had quickly got used to working with these stars and we were never in awe of them, but I think we were all secretly excited about meeting Frank Sinatra. It seemed like the whole of London was. The day his run was due to start I arrived at the theatre for rehearsals and there was already a huge crowd gathered outside the stage door hoping to get a glimpse of him.

'Excuse me, excuse me,' I shouted, trying to push my way past the big group of hysterical fans.

'Are you working with Mr Sinatra?' a woman shouted.

'Yes, I will be,' I said. 'That's if I can get in the stage door.'

I finally managed to fight my way into the theatre.

'Blimey, it's pandemonium out there,' I said to George the doorman.

'It's crazy,' he told me. 'Some of them have been there since the early hours. We've had to request a police escort to get Mr Sinatra in and out of the theatre.'

There was no such thing as bodyguards or security staff in those days, and most stars just travelled with their partner and sometimes their manager. We'd never seen anything like this before.

It wasn't just the public who were excited. The whole cast and crew were buzzing about the arrival of Ol' Blue Eyes. We were in the midst of rehearsals that afternoon, and as we ran through our routine one last time and danced off stage we saw a group of people standing in the wings.

'Oh, Lordy, it's Frank Sinatra,' gasped Anne. 'He's here.'

We all craned our necks to try to catch a glimpse of him as he was being introduced to the backstage staff. He was in his thirties and an older man compared with us girls. He had a reputation of being a bit of a womaniser, and I could see why.

'He's much more handsome in real life,' I whispered.

Jack the stage manager brought him over to where we were standing.

'And here are the Palladium Tiller Girls, who will be opening and closing the show for you,' he said.

We were all completely star-struck and just stood there like lemons with big grins on our faces.

'Hello, ladies,' he said. 'I'm looking forward to seeing you in action.'

'Hello, Mr Sinatra,' we all chorused.

'Isn't he small?' whispered Peggy as he wandered off to meet the stage-hands.

I too had expected him to be taller somehow, and most of the girls towered over him.

'He's not much bigger than me,' I said.

He can't have been any more than five foot seven, and on stage I think he must have worn shoes with a bit of a wedged heel to make him look taller.

The excitement was building for his first night and the atmosphere in the theatre was electric. It was standing room only in the stalls, and the minute the curtain went back to reveal Mr Sinatra reclining on a velvet chaise-longue the audience erupted. We could hear the whoops, cheers and whistles all the way up to our dressing-room as he belted out over a dozen songs.

All of us girls had autograph books that we always got the big stars to sign, and we couldn't pass up the opportunity to get Frank Sinatra in there.

'Someone needs to take them to his dressing-room in one go so he can do them all at once,' said Peggy.

'I can't do it,' said Sylvia. 'I'm too nervous.'

'I'm worried I'll make a fool of myself or say something stupid,' said Anne.

'Oh, give them here,' I said. 'Jean and I

will go.'

Before now I'd never really been in awe of any of the stars. We all just treated them as part of the show and got on with it. But I felt very excited and a little bit nervous as we headed to Frank Sinatra's dressing-room. In those days all the stars used the same basic dressing-rooms, starkly furnished with just a wooden table and chair. There were none of the ridiculous requests that so-called celebrities have today, like painting the room white and having scented candles everywhere or a bath filled with champagne. If anyone had asked for things like that in our day they would have been laughed at.

I must admit my hands were shaking as I knocked on the door.

'Come in, girls,' smiled Frank when he saw us standing there.

'We wondered whether you'd be so kind as to sign our autograph books, Mr Sinatra?' I asked.

'Of course,' he said. 'I'd be delighted.'

Jean and I stood there with silly grins on our faces while he signed our pile of twenty-five books.

'Thank you so much, Mr Sinatra,' said Jean, practically bowing. 'That's very kind of you. The girls will be pleased.'

'My pleasure, ladies,' he said.

We were both in awe, having got up close and personal with someone who was considered such a big star and who was so friendly. As we came out we passed a woman walking down the corridor. She was a tiny little thing, but absolutely stunning and very glamorous with her green eyes, dark curly hair and luscious red lips.

'It's Ava Gardner,' whispered Jean.

She was going out with Sinatra at the time and was obviously on her way to see him.

Everyone screamed when we got back to our dressing-room with the books.

'What was he like?' Peggy asked.

'He's so charming and sweet,' sighed Jean. 'He made my legs turn to jelly.'

'And did you see his eyes?' I said. 'They really are the most amazing colour.'

Of course, I knew that his nickname was Ol' Blue Eyes, but when you saw him in the flesh you realised why. They were a really striking violet blue colour like hyacinths.

That night, last out as usual, I was shocked when I pushed open the stage door to find a huge crowd of people waiting at the bottom of the stairs.

I went back in to see George.

'I don't believe it, it's still mobbed out there,' I said.

'They're all waiting for Mr Sinatra, even though he went hours ago through a different exit. Do you want me to clear a way for you?'

'No, it's OK,' I said. 'I'll fight my way out.'

But as soon as I went out, the crowd

surged forward.

'Miss, Miss,' they shouted. 'Have you been working with Frank Sinatra?'

'Yes, I have,' I said, desperately trying to get through so I could catch the last Tube from Oxford Circus. 'But sadly I think he left the theatre a while ago.'

'Miss, what's he like?' someone else shouted.

'He's very charming,' I said. 'And very handsome, of course.'

Frank Sinatra took the whole country by storm. After a two-week sell-out run at the Palladium he went up to Blackpool and performed two concerts at the New Opera House.

We got to know some of the big stars better than others and often we'd chat to them during rehearsals. One of these was the singer and comedian Jimmy Durante, who was a really nice man. He was known for his big, bulbous nose, which he used to jokingly call his 'schnozzola' – and it became his nickname. In fact on all the posters advertising his run at the Palladium he was billed as the 'Great Schnozzola'. We had to do a special dance routine with him in which we were all dressed as bobby-soxers, which was a popular fashion for young girls at that time. We wore poodle skirts, woollen hats and little white ankle socks.

Jimmy came to see us before rehearsals.

'Girls, I've got a bit of a problem and I wondered if you could help me,' he said in his gravelly New York accent.

'Yes, Mr Durante,' we said.

'Please call me Jimmy,' he told us. 'You see, the thing is, ladies, my eyesight is terrible but I can't wear glasses on the stage as they'll reflect the lights.

'Do you think you can just let me know when I need to go on and come off, as I can't see the stage manager?'

We agreed to help, but when we started rehearsing it was clear he couldn't see more than two feet in front of his enormous nose.

'He's as blind as a bat,' whispered Sylvia.

When the music started he didn't have a clue, as he just stood there even though Jack was waving frantically to him. I danced over to the side of the stage.

'It's time to go on, Jimmy,' I whispered, pulling him onto the stage by his suit tails.

We danced either side of him while he stood in the middle and sang. But, of course, he missed his cue to exit the stage at the end of our routine.

'Jimmy, it's time to get off,' I hissed, pushing him onto the side of the stage.

Every night we did the same thing. Whoever was nearest to him would have to haul him on and push him off, often quite forcibly, but he didn't seem to mind.

'You're marvellous, girls,' he said. 'I don't

know what I'd do without you.'

'He could try and get himself some better glasses that don't reflect the light,' whispered Anne.

At the end of the fortnight run, his manager came into our dressing-room to see us.

'This is from Jimmy to say thanks,' he told us all, and he handed each of us a £5 note.

It was a heck of a lot of money in those days and we were overwhelmed.

'What a nice man,' I said.

We found out later that he'd gone around the theatre giving everyone money. Everybody from the cleaners right up to the stage manager got something from him to say thank you.

'I bet it's all a tax dodge,' one of the Skyrockets told me. 'Rumour has it that he's given thousands of pounds away so he doesn't have to pay it in tax.'

Whether it was a tax dodge or not, I was thrilled with my fiver, which I used to buy a wooden bookcase. It's still standing now, over sixty years later, and I always think of Jimmy Durante when I look at it.

The Palladium also played host to many black stars from the US, like Winifred Atwell, the Nicholas Brothers and Nat King Cole, who was such a gentleman and so polite. I was especially taken with the actress and singer Lena Horne. She was stunningly beautiful and a lovely person too, and she always came to sit with us during rehearsals.

'I love watching you girls dance,' she said. 'If ever you need anything or there's something you're not happy with, then just let me or my manager know.'

She was a well-known civil rights activist and fought against racism in the entertainment industry. I really admired her for this.

'Unfortunately racism is rife in the US,' she told us. 'If I was performing there then I wouldn't be allowed to use the same bathrooms or dressing-rooms as the white performers.

'It's nice to come to this country where we're treated just the same as any other performer.'

I was absolutely horrified. No wonder these stars wanted to perform in London, where everyone was treated the same and they were welcomed with open arms.

But not all of the stars were so friendly. I was looking forward to seeing the American entertainer Bob Hope, as he always made me laugh, but when he came over for his run he wouldn't talk to anybody and was very aloof.

On his first night, with only minutes to go before he was due on stage, there was no sign of him.

'Where is Mr Hope?' yelled Jack, who was tearing his hair out and pacing up and down backstage.

'I think he's playing golf,' said one of the stage-hands.

'Golf?' gasped Jack, practically having a heart attack. 'Does he not realise there's two thousand people waiting out there to see him?'

His opening music was starting when someone shouted from backstage: 'Here he is!'

And literally as the last note sounded, Bob Hope appeared and with not a word to anyone casually walked onto the stage to begin his act.

'Poor Jack was having kittens back there,' said Peggy.

Jack just looked relieved as he gave the signal to pull back the curtains for the second half to begin.

The same thing happened every night. Bob Hope would spend all day at the golf course and he'd time it perfectly so that just as his overture was playing he would walk into the theatre and go straight onto the stage. Then he would simply do his act and disappear.

'I haven't seen him speak to anybody,' I said.

'How rude,' said one of the stage-hands.

But in general the big stars were very quiet and down to earth. There was no such thing as instant fame or celebrity in those days. Most of them had worked their way up and had been learning their craft for years before hitting the big time.

But not all of the Hollywood stars went down a storm. Bud Abbott and Lou Costello, for example, had been booked to top the bill for two weeks. They were huge film stars, known for their slapstick comedy routines that were like Laurel and Hardy. They were hilarious on film, but it was a different kettle of fish when it came to live theatre. They were an absolute disaster. We knew there was something wrong, as usually the roar of the Palladium crowd carried right up to our dressing-room in the attic and made the walls shake. But that night we couldn't hear a thing.

'What happened?' I asked Jack after the show.

'They were an absolute wash-out,' he told me. 'They completely bombed.'

I felt sorry for the comedians as they really had to prove themselves. Whenever the Tillers appeared on stage we were always well received and got a big round of applause, but the funny men had to work hard to win the audience over and they could die a death out there. Poor Abbott and Costello only lasted a week, and Val Parnell was panicking about their replacement. He came into the dressing-room to see us one day.

'I want you girls to audition a new comedian for me,' he said.

So we all trooped down to the auditorium and took a seat in the front row.

'Let me know what you think, ladies,' said Mr Parnell.

The new guy was called Max Bygraves and he was a carpenter in his late twenties who had been in the RAF during the war. Val Parnell had discovered him working in a little suburban theatre. He was very funny and endearing, and we were laughing away. At the end of his act we all whooped and cheered, and gave him a standing ovation.

'Well, girls,' said Vat Parnell. 'What do you think?'

'He was great,' said Peggy.

'I thought he was wonderful,' I told him.

It was a bit of a risk putting a British un-known at the top of the bill, but Max Bygraves replaced Abbott and Costello for the final week of their run. He went down a storm and he became a star overnight. Sadly he died a couple of years ago, but as I've always said I hope he knew that his big break came when he was auditioned by the Palladium Tiller Girls!

The supporting artists were usually people who had been performing in variety shows around the country for years. There were lots of trapeze artists and tumblers, singers and jugglers, and acts like Wilson, Keppel and Betty – two lanky men with moustaches and a woman who had done exactly the same sandman routine for donkey's years. This involved them sprinkling sand on the stage and doing a comical shuffling Egyptian dance. The strangest one was three former SS soldiers from Germany who sprayed themselves in gold-leaf paint and did a balancing act. They didn't speak a word of English and none of us girls had seen anything like it before in our lives.

'They're so tall and strapping,' gasped Peggy.

'And they've got nothing on but jock straps,' winked Jean.

The Palladium corridors were so narrow and they were so huge, that when we passed them on the way back up to the dressing-room we had to flatten ourselves against the wall so they could squeeze past.

It was very rare for us to ever see the stars perform ourselves, but we got lucky once during a break between American variety seasons, when Judy Garland was performing at the Palladium.

'I'll make sure all you Tiller Girls get tickets,' Jack told us.

He kept his word, and one night we sat there in the audience waiting for her to come on stage.

'Isn't it funny seeing things from this side?' said Peggy.

We were all excited when the orchestra started playing her overture, but after a couple of minutes they stopped.

'Something's wrong,' I whispered.

Then the music started again but a few minutes later the same thing happened and it stopped. I could just imagine Jack panicking backstage. The band stopped and started three times before Judy Garland finally arrived on stage. It was an amazing performance, and the standing ovation she got at the end was one of the loudest and longest that I'd ever seen in all of the time that I'd worked there.

'What was all that about?' we asked Jack later when we nipped backstage.

'Miss Garland was refusing to come out of her dressing-room,' he sighed.

'You poor thing,' I said. 'I bet you were tearing your hair out.'

'You can say that again,' he said. 'Thankfully her manager managed to persuade her in the end.'

We heard through the grapevine later that it was because she had been blotto. I was amazed, though, as her performance when she'd finally got on stage had been absolutely flawless.

'Poor woman,' I sighed. 'She's obviously a very troubled soul.'

Everyone knew that she'd had problems with drugs and alcohol, and a year earlier she'd slashed her wrists after her film contract with MGM had been cancelled.

It wasn't often you saw celebrities in the audience rather than on stage, but that happened while I was performing at the London Casino. A few of us Tiller Girls had been sent to appear in a production of *Aladdin*, with Nat Jackley as Widow Twanky and Julie Andrews as the princess. In the opening scene we played Chinese villagers and I had to walk on stage in my long robe wearing a big straw hat and carrying a bird in a cage. On the first night I was standing by the front cloth, which is the area on the very edge of the stage just where the curtain closes and where the lights are. I was singing along to the opening number when I looked out into the audience and caught the eye of a gentleman in the front row. When I realised who he was I did a double take.

Crikey, it's Orson Welles, I told myself.

There he was, one of the most famous actors in the world, and he was staring straight at me. He looked a bit puzzled. I think maybe as an American he hadn't been to an English pantomime before and he was a bit bemused by the whole thing. He was putting me off, so I tried to look somewhere else, but he still kept staring at me!

'Did you see who that was?' I said to the girls after we came off stage. 'Orson Welles was sat there in the front row.'

They all had a peep around the curtain to try to get a glimpse of him.

I'd got used to working with some of the world's biggest names on a daily basis, but even I was allowed to get a little star-struck from time to time.

12

Disaster Strikes

Things don't always run smoothly in the theatre – like life, I suppose – and little did we know there were a few obstacles coming our way.

The first happened during Monday morning rehearsals when we were going through a new routine for the last two weeks of the season that involved us splitting up and forming two circles. We were twirling around on the stage when suddenly I heard a bang and a yelp.

'What's happened?' said Miss Barbara, raising her hand to interrupt the pianist.

Anne, who was one of the shortest girls, was lying on the floor writhing in agony.

'I lost my balance and tripped over,' she moaned. 'I think I've hurt my ribs.'

We managed to help lift her up off the floor.

'Did you not use the rosin box, dear?' Miss

Barbara asked.

'I'm so sorry, I forgot,' she said.

The rosin box was a little box full of yellow crystals that was always at the side of the stage. When you stepped into it, the crystals turned into a sticky white powder and coated the bottom of your dance shoes to stop you from slipping over on the stage.

Poor Anne was in agony after her fall.

'I think you need to go to hospital, dear, and get checked over,' Miss Doris told her. 'You go with her, Kay.'

They came back later that afternoon.

'She's cracked her ribs,' said Kay, helping her into the dressing-room.

'You poor thing,' I said. 'You must be in agony.'

'Anne, you should go home and rest,' Sylvia told her. 'You can't dance with cracked ribs.'

But she shook her head.

'They strapped them up so I should be OK for tonight's shows,' she said bravely. 'I'll just try and carry on as normal.'

I could tell she was still in a lot of pain and she was struggling to walk, never mind dance, but I knew that she was terrified about losing her place in the troupe. That was our worst fear and none of us wanted to be replaced.

We were all in the dressing-room getting ready for that evening's first show when a short, tubby woman in her forties came in to see us.

'Hello there, girls,' she said. 'My name's Nessie and I'm the West End Equity rep.'

The trade union Equity had been going since the 1930s but it had only recently opened up its membership to dancers in variety shows, pantomimes and ballets. Nessie's job was to wander round all the theatres in the West End persuading performers to pay their subs and join.

'You'll find most performers in West End theatres have union membership,' she told us. 'It's highly advisable to protect yourselves.'

'That's all well and good, but what do we get out of it?' asked Sylvia.

'It means that all your jobs and future contracts will be looked at and vetted by Equity,' she said. 'I'm sure you've all heard of dancers being sent abroad and being exploited, or having contracts cancelled or breached? It means that all your contracts from now on will be Equity-approved. Have a think about it and I'll come back tomorrow.'

It cost a half crown a week to join and we were all a bit fidgety about shelling out for it.

'Well, my loyalty is to Tillers,' said Jean. 'What are Miss Barbara and Miss Doris going to say? They might not like us joining a union.'

'Come on, girls,' said Anne. 'I think we're being a bit naïve here. We're not going to be at the Palladium for ever, and we need to protect ourselves when we go and find other jobs.'

'I think she's right,' said Sylvia. 'My friend Constance knows a girl who was sent out to Turkey to dance in a show, but when she got there they wanted her to perform topless and there were all sorts of seedy goings on. She was practically treated like a lady of the night.'

We'd all heard horror stories of young girls like us sent out to foreign countries to work who would find themselves stuck in danger-ous situations but were unable to afford their ticket home.

'Do you think it's a good idea, Irene?' Kay asked me.

'I think so,' I said.

My political background had taught me that unions were a good thing and gave power to the ordinary people.

So, despite us being a little unsure, when Nessie came back to see us the next day we all paid our two shillings and sixpence, and became Equity members.

'We're currently campaigning for an industry-wide ruling to increase chorus girls' wages,' she told us. 'So if you want to come and join the picket line then let us know.'

None of us did, as we didn't want to rock

the boat, and we knew that it would probably be frowned on by Miss Barbara and Miss Doris.

'Just imagine their faces if we told them we were going on strike!' said Ruth.

'I think we'd all be looking for a new job,' replied Jean.

Although we weren't exactly making our fortunes we were all getting paid £20 a week, which I thought was a decent enough wage.

A fortnight later we heard that Equity had won its fight and there was going to be a wage increase for chorus girls like us to £25 a week. It was going to be across the board and all of the theatres in the West End had to comply with the ruling.

'Well, we can't complain about Equity if they've got us a pay rise,' I said.

But the next day, when we arrived at the Palladium for rehearsals, Miss Barbara and Miss Doris were waiting in our dressing-room with stern faces.

'Mr Parnell would like to see you all in the auditorium,' said Miss Doris.

We all looked at each other in a panic and I just knew instinctively that something was wrong.

'Summat's up, that's for sure,' said Brenda in her thick northern accent.

We all trooped down there along with Miss Barbara and Miss Doris, and took a seat. Val

Parnell stood up and cleared his throat.

'Good morning, girls,' he said. 'I wanted to talk to you as there's been a bit of a change in our plans. For business reasons we will now only need twenty girls in the show.

'So, after discussions with Miss Barbara and Miss Doris, I'm afraid I'm going to have to let five of you dancers go.'

We all sat there in shock at what we were hearing.

My heart started racing and I felt sick. I didn't want to leave; not now, not like this. I loved working at the Palladium. All of us did. We watched intently as Val Parnell got a piece of paper out of his pocket.

Please don't let it be me, I thought selfishly to myself.

'So Edith, Anne, Molly, Kathleen and Margaret, please go and get your things from the dressing-room and leave the theatre,' he said. 'Thank you for your contribution, ladies, and I wish you every success for the future.'

As he walked off we all looked at each other completely stunned. Anne burst into tears and the rest of the girls just looked shell-shocked.

'I can't believe this is happening,' Anne sobbed. The poor girl was still in agony with her cracked ribs.

None of us could believe it.

Miss Barbara and Miss Doris looked

upset too.

'I'm so sorry, girls, there was nothing we could do,' said Miss Doris. 'Our hands our tied. If we want to keep our contract with the Palladium then we have to keep the management happy.'

'I know it doesn't make it any easier, but it was purely a business decision,' Miss Barbara told us. 'It's nothing personal.'

We knew that they had a right to terminate our contracts at any time, but it was still such a shock. I was so relieved that I wasn't leaving, but I also felt upset and terribly guilty that I could stay.

'This is all probably because of the Equity ruling so they don't have to increase their wage bill,' I whispered to Jean.

We'd all got a pay rise to £25 a week but if there were five fewer girls on the payroll then it meant the management was still paying out the same amount each week in wages.

The girls who were going looked absolutely devastated, especially Anne, who was inconsolable.

'I'm going to miss you all so much,' she sobbed, giving us all a hug.

'I'm so sorry,' I said.

Half an hour later all five girls were gone. It had all happened so quickly

'What about the line?' asked Jean. 'Won't it look odd without these five girls?'

'Well, we'll all just have to squash up a bit on stage and we shouldn't notice too much,' said Kay. 'I'll call rehearsals so we can make sure that our routines aren't affected.'

It was going to feel strange dancing with only twenty of us in the line. I knew the girls who'd left would have no trouble finding work, but they would be hard pressed to find something that matched up to being part of the Tillers' top troupe at the London Palladium. In a way it made us all count our blessings and remember how lucky we were to be there.

But that wasn't the only bombshell the week had in store. A few days later I was at home in the living-room when I reached down to get a book and a sharp pain shot through my back. When I tried to stand up again I realised I couldn't.

'Somebody help me!' I yelled, panicking. 'I can't straighten up.'

Eventually Mum heard me shouting and came to see what all the fuss was about.

'Something's happened,' I wailed. 'I'm bent double and I can't get up.'

'Oh, Rene, dear, I think your back's gone,' she said. 'It'll be all those years of dancing.'

I'd never had any trouble with my back before, not even any pain or twinges, but now I was stooped over like the Hunchback of Notre Dame. With Mum's help I managed to straighten up a little bit and she helped me over to an armchair.

'I'd better get you an appointment with Dr Miller,' she said.

Only a few weeks earlier, in July 1948, the National Health Service had been created, and thankfully it meant that you didn't have to pay to see the doctor any more. I managed to hobble down to Dr Miller's surgery on Northcote Road, and he took one look at me and referred me to the Royal National Orthopaedic Hospital in Great Portland Street in the West End. I felt sick, as this sounded serious and I knew there was no way I was going to be able to dance in the show that night.

'I've never had a day off sick before,' I told Mum.

But I was terrified that if they knew it was serious they would find someone to replace me. I rang the Palladium office and told them I wouldn't be in that night.

'I'm sure it's nothing and I'll be back to-morrow as normal,' I said.

We didn't have a swing, which is what an understudy is called in the dancing world, who could step in if we were ill. It hardly ever happened, so we normally just shifted up the line a bit.

Mum had to go and play in the orchestra that night, so I had to get a taxi to the hospital as there was no way I could walk very far.

'I hope it's nothing serious,' I said to the specialist as he examined me.

'What do you do for a living?' he asked me.

'I'm a dancer,' I told him. 'I'm a Tiller Girl at the London Palladium.'

'Ah, I see,' he said, pressing down my spine.

I just wanted to know what treatment I needed, and then get the heck out of there and back to work. I hated hospitals. They reminded me of my father and going to see him when he had TB, as well as the time I had an abscess in my ear.

'Well, Miss Starr,' he told me finally. 'I think you've slipped a disc in your back.'

'What does that mean?' I asked.

'You'll need to be in plaster for six weeks from under your armpits down to your hip bone,' he said. 'And I'm afraid even if your back does eventually recover it's unlikely that you'll ever be able to dance again.'

'Pardon me?' I said, not really taking in what I was hearing.

'I know it will be a huge blow to you, but I really don't think that you'll be dancing again,' he said.

'No offence, doctor, but that's complete and utter bobbins,' I told him.

Dancing was my greatest passion in life. In many ways it *was* my life, and the thought of not being able to do it any more was un-imaginable. I was very angry, and basically told him to go and get knotted.

212

It brought out the stubborn streak in me. Even now, if I'm told that I can't do something I become all the more determined to do it. Nothing and no one, especially not some silly doctor, was going to stop me from dancing. I didn't believe what he was telling me for one second.

Just the thought of being in plaster for six weeks was unbearable enough for me. I was always such a busy, active person and I hated doing nothing.

I lay there while the nurse wound the wet bandages around me.

'Now, you'll just have to lie there while the cast dries and hardens,' she said.

The doctor had manipulated my back slightly and although I was still in pain, I had straightened up and at least I could walk.

I knew that there was no way I could dance in a body cast, though, and I was worried to death about what I was going to tell Tillers. I phoned Miss Barbara as soon as I got home.

'I'm so sorry, but I've slipped a disc in my back and I don't think I'm going to be able to dance for a few weeks,' I told her nervously.

'Don't worry, dear,' she said. 'In a way it couldn't have happened at a better time.'

It was true. An American stars season was just coming to an end, and then there was a two-month break before another production came to the Palladium. All the girls were being sent off around the country to do summer seasons. 'While they're doing that it means that you can rest so you get yourself right for next season,' she said.

'Oh, thank you, Miss Barbara,' I said, my voice light with relief. 'I was so worried that you were going to replace me.'

'Don't be silly, dear,' she said. 'Just keep in touch, and let myself or Miss Doris know when you'll be back.'

I'd just refused point blank to believe what the doctor told me about never dancing again and I was determined to get back to the Palladium as soon as possible. I was absolutely bored stiff at home doing nothing. Mum and Harry had gone away on tour and the weather was lovely, but I couldn't go anywhere as I had to rest my back.

One day Sylvia came to see me before she went down to Brighton to do the summer season.

'How are you getting on, Irene?' she asked.

'Oh, Sylv, it's sooo boring,' I said. 'I can't have a bath, so I just have to have a top and tail wash. And this cast is so itchy.'

'Here, take one of my knitting needles and have a good scratch,' she said.

It felt like heaven as I shoved one of the needles down my cast.

I was constantly boiling hot with that heavy

cast on, and I lost so much weight that I could turn around inside it.

'Keep your spirits up, Irene, and I'll see you soon,' said Sylvia.

'Don't you worry, I'll be back soon,' I told her.

I hated every second of resting. Two months later I was so pleased when I went back to the hospital and had my cast cut off with what looked like a circular saw. My back felt fine and I practically skipped home.

I couldn't wait to get back to work and start dancing again. A new American stars variety season wasn't starting until the New Year, but it meant that I could start rehearsing for the annual Royal Command Performance that was taking place in November. But a couple of days into rehearsals I was in the dressing-room warming up when my back went again.

'Oh, good God, no!' I wailed.

'What is it, Irene?' Brenda asked.

'It's my back,' I said. 'I think it's gone again. This can't be happening.'

I was so anxious at the thought that that the silly doctor had been right.

'You should go and see an osteopath, Irene,' Brenda told me. 'Some people do say they're quacks, but I know a few dancers who say it's worked miracles for them.'

Osteopaths were rare in those days and tended to be disapproved of by the medical profession. There was only one practice in

215

the whole of south-west London – a Swedish brother and sister who worked near Clapham Common.

I got a taxi from the Palladium and hobbled back to see Dr Miller.

'My back's gone again, but instead of going to the hospital this time I'm going to go and see an osteopath,' I told him.

His face fell.

'I'm afraid I can't condone that, Miss Starr,' he said. 'In fact, I would strongly advise against it, and if you do see one then I will have to strike you off my register.'

'Well, so be it then,' I told him.

I couldn't face the thought of being put in another plaster cast and being told that I wasn't going to dance again. I still refused to believe such a gloomy prognosis for a second, and there was no way on earth I was going to miss the Royal Command Performance.

So I went to see the Swedish brother and sister osteopaths. I was only in there fifteen minutes and they worked on me together.

'Your back is misaligned because of all the dancing,' they said.

A few clicks here and there, and I came walking out as straight as a die. I never had any back problems again.

'Brenda, you were right,' I said. 'It's a miracle.'

It felt wonderful to be back at work doing what I loved and we were all very excited about our first Royal Command Perform-ance, which was what the Royal Variety Show was called in those days. Danny Kaye was headlining, and it was the first time in history that an American star had been asked to top the bill of the country's most prestigious show.

It was being held on a wet Monday night in November, but as I arrived at the theatre early that evening nothing could dampen my spirits. A thrill of excitement ran through me as I saw the big banner on the front of the building that declared: 'Tonight – Royal Command Performance in the presence of their majesties the King and Queen'. All of the brass door handles and the gilt mirrors in the foyer were gleaming after a good polish, and it smelled lovely as it was decked out with huge arrangements of beautiful roses.

It was a very different atmosphere back-stage too. Everyone was rushing about, and they all looked very nervous and stressed. All of us Tiller Girls were just very excited as we got ready in our dressing-room.

A couple of us decided to sneak down-stairs and have a peep out of the front windows.

'Look at the crowd outside,' gasped Jean.

There were literally hundreds of people crammed into Argyll Street in the rain hop-ing to catch a glimpse of a famous star or the King and Queen as they arrived. They were being watched over by policemen on horseback, and in front of the theatre stood a line of officers in rain capes holding the crowds back.

We watched, fascinated, as two commissionaires rolled the plush red carpet down the marble staircase and onto the wet pavement. They secured it with brass stair rods and started to brush it down.

'Pity the poor person who leaves a wet footprint on that,' I laughed.

Two doormen were holding huge umbrellas to try to shield the glamorous guests from the weather as they arrived. We stared in awe at the specially invited audience – handsome men in dinner suits and women in long evening dresses draped in furs.

'Come on, Jean, enough of the gawping. We'd better go and get ready,' I said. 'We can't be late for the King and Queen.'

We didn't need a shout from the call boy that evening. We could hear the huge cheer from the crowd all the way up in our dressing-room as the King and Queen pulled up outside.

'Quick,' said Kay, 'they've arrived. We'd better get down there.'

According to tradition, the royal family were the last people to enter the auditorium and everyone else had to be seated when they came in. As we all filed down the stairs and waited in the wings I couldn't resist pulling back the side curtain a teeny bit and having a nosey. The Palladium always looked grand, but it looked even more spectacular tonight with fresh flowers covering the front of the royal box and the audience in all their finery.

'They've really spruced the place up,' said Peggy. 'Apparently they've even got posh loo roll in the toilets with the royal crest stamped on it.'

We were first on stage and we started to feel really nervous as we stood in the wings. It wasn't helped by the fact that all the backstage staff were on edge.

'No mistakes tonight, please, girls,' said Jack, who was pacing up and down clutching his clipboard. 'Everything's got to be perfect.'

'Keep your hair on,' I joked. 'Don't worry, we'll make you proud.'

Suddenly a hush descended over the audience and the band started to play the National Anthem. Everyone stood up as the royal family made their entrance. King George and Queen Elizabeth came in first, followed by Princess Elizabeth and the Duke of Edinburgh, who were due to celebrate their first wedding anniversary in a couple of weeks.

'Ooh, don't they look beautiful,' gasped Peggy. 'Look at their lovely dresses.'

The Queen wore a dazzling diamond tiara, a white ermine cape and a long white satin dress with flowers embroidered onto it. Princess Elizabeth looked stunning in a pink satin dress and a cape matching her mother's. But there was no time to stare.

'Take your positions please, girls,' we heard Jack say. 'Curtain up in ten seconds.'

'Oh, sweet Jesus, I hope we don't cock it up,' said Jean.

'We won't,' I said. 'We can't.'

We were all unusually nervous and on edge because of the expectation and pressure of the occasion. We knew there was a packed house of the great and the good sitting out there in their finery, and the royal family watching us from their box. We always strove for perfection, but tonight we knew that everything had to be absolutely flawless. Our reputations, as well as those of Miss Barbara and Miss Doris, were at stake.

We all lined up at the back of the stage in our outfits that had been specially made for that night's performance – white embroidered satin tunic tops that flared out from the waist and had a big split up the front to show off our tight white knickers, and hats with feathery pompoms on the top that shimmied as we moved.

'Deep breaths, girls,' said Sylvia.

Jack gave us the nod and a second later the Skyrockets launched into a lively number.

Our fast and furious routine had been expressly choreographed by Miss Barbara to show off our kicking skills. Perfectly in time to the music, we did a dozen shoots – which was the term that we used for low scissor kicks – while we moved to the back of the stage, then another twelve shoots forward. Our feathery pompoms fluttered as we turned our heads left and right and back again in perfect unison. What followed was a complex mix of high kicks and circle kicks ending in what we called a wheel – where the central girl didn't move but the rest of us circled around her as if she were on a pivot. We finished off the routine with seven high kicks and then, on the eighth count, we all dropped down onto the floor on our left knees with our right knees out in front of us. The audience erupted after our dramatic finale, but there was no time to lap up the applause or enjoy our moment of glory in front of all those dignitaries. We jumped up and, with a quick bow to the royal box, we high-kicked our way off stage left. Only then did I allow myself to finally breathe.

'Thank God that's over,' I gasped.

'We did so well,' said Peggy. 'The audience seemed to love it.'

I still had the same buzz and adrenalin rush, but it was more relief than exhilaration that I felt that night as we ran up the stairs to our dressing-room.

'Bravo, girls,' said Miss Barbara when she came up to see us. 'That was just perfect. Not even a hair out of place.'

We kicked off a bill that included tumblers, acrobats, midgets, comedians, several bands and a thirteen-year-old girl soprano.

We opened up the second half with a military-style dance for which we were all dressed like soldiers, and then it was time for Danny Kaye, who was top of the bill. As always, the audience went crazy for him. At the end the whole cast came on stage to sing the National Anthem, and bow or curtsey to the King and Queen. Miss Barbara had reminded us of the protocol.

'Everyone will turn stage left towards the royal box but don't look at the Queen,' she said.

'Why?' asked Jean. 'Will we get put in prison?'

'You'll get taken to the Tower,' I whispered.

Afterwards, while we traipsed upstairs back to our dressing-room, the other stars lined up in the foyer to meet the royal family.

'Bloody cheek,' grumbled Jean. 'We were in the show too. Why can't we meet the King and Queen?'

We were all a bit miffed that we weren't allowed to meet the royals but I knew we weren't the big stars; in the pecking order of the show we were probably somewhere near the bottom.

But one person who definitely wasn't keen on the royal family was my brother Raymond.

'It's about time I came to see you dance at the Palladium, Rene,' he said one day.

I was so pleased, as none of my family had ever seen me perform before, and it was very sweet of him as he wasn't really a theatre man. He much preferred going to the cinema or having his head buried in a book.

'I'll get you a ticket to one of the shows in the new variety season,' I told him.

So a few weeks later he came to a matinée.

'My brother's out there watching tonight,' I told all the other girls proudly.

'There he is,' I said, pointing him out in the second row.

As was customary before any performance in the Forties and Fifties, the band played the National Anthem and the whole auditorium stood up to sing 'God Save the King'. Everyone, that was, except my brother.

I could have died when I looked through the curtain and saw two thousand people on their feet except him in the second row. I prayed no one would notice, as I was so embarrassed. But unfortunately he stuck out like a sore thumb and people were staring at him being so disrespectful.

''Ere, Irene, what's that brother of yours playing at?' laughed Jean.

'Why isn't he standing up like everyone else?' asked Brenda.

'Put it this way,' I said. 'He's not that keen on the royals.'

I was so cross I could have killed him. The Palladium was my special place, and it felt as if he'd come in and spoilt it for me. I was mortified that people had noticed.

He was waiting for me when I came out of the theatre with a big grin on his face.

'I'm so angry with you, Raymond,' I told him. 'You sat down for the National Anthem.'

'Of course I did, Rene,' he said. 'You know I'm an anti-royalist.'

'Well, it was really embarrassing,' I said.

I was well and truly miffed that for once in his life he couldn't forget his principles, even for my sake.

He didn't have a clue about dancing and he never said what he thought of the show. To him, I think, I was always going to be his slightly silly, dizzy baby sister.

13

Making Mum Proud

We all gathered in the dressing-room as we'd been told Miss Doris had an important announcement to make.

'Girls, I've got some very exciting news,' she said.

We all looked at each other in anticipation.

'Tillers have been invited to go on a twelve-week tour of South Africa,' she told us. 'It's a huge honour for us to be asked to go and perform over there, and as you're the top troupe I wanted you to be the ones to go.'

Everyone was jumping up and down and squealing with excitement.

'I can't believe it,' said Kay. 'I've always dreamed of going to Africa.'

'Do you think there will be lions and tigers?' said Jean. 'Oh, Lord, I hope we don't get eaten.

'Isn't it exciting, Irene?'

But I just shrugged.

'I'm not going to South Africa,' I told her. 'I can't.'

'Why ever not?' she asked. 'It's going to be wonderful.'

'I can't go somewhere where they've got apartheid,' I said.

I'd read in the newspapers about what had been going on over there since apartheid had been recently introduced and I'd been horrified. I knew I couldn't dance and act all jolly knowing that black South Africans weren't allowed to sit in the theatre where we were performing or go into the same café or use the same toilets as us just because of the colour of their skin.

'You'd better tell Miss Barbara and Miss Doris, then,' she whispered.

Unsurprisingly, they weren't best pleased that I was refusing to go.

'Irene, I don't think you realise what a fantastic opportunity this is,' said Miss Doris. 'It's a big coup for Tillers to be invited over there.'

'I know,' I said. 'I just don't want to be part of it. I wouldn't feel comfortable.'

They tried to get me to reconsider, but I was having none of it.

'I will not go to a country where they treat their own people like that,' I said firmly. 'It's completely against everything that I believe in.'

I was a stubborn little thing once I'd made my mind up about something.

'Well, I'm very disappointed,' said Miss Barbara. 'It's not good for troupe morale to have one of our best dancers not accompanying us. We shall have to find somewhere else for you to go, of course, while the rest of the girls are away.'

I could tell they were cross with me, but nothing was going to change my mind. I'd been shocked by what some of the black American stars had told me about how they had been treated in their own country, and I knew South Africa was much worse. It was a step too far for me and I refused point blank.

The other girls didn't really understand it.

'Oh, Irene, you're so political,' said Jean. 'You'll be missing out.'

'There's nothing wrong with having a strong opinion,' I told her.

It was hard seeing them getting all excited about going somewhere so exotic, and on a plane as well, but I knew in my heart I just couldn't have gone. Thankfully my mother and my brother understood.

'It's your political upbringing kicking in,' Mum told me. 'You don't like to see any injustice, just like your father.'

While everyone else was packing for South Africa I found out what my punishment was for not toeing the line – a summer season in Great Yarmouth. It was in a little theatre, and I was on the bill with five girls from another Tiller troupe who were based at the Victoria Palace.

'You must be mad,' one of them told me.

227

'Performing here every day when you could be in Africa.'

'You need your head testing,' another one said.

But I knew in my heart that I'd made the right decision. It would have gone against all my principles.

The girls came back in the autumn but, to my shock, two of them were missing.

'Where's Kay and Iris?' I asked.

'They're engaged to be married,' said Peggy excitedly. 'The men were flocking round us out there, Irene.'

They'd both been swept off their feet by South African men and had decided to stay out there.

'Oh, it was amazing, Irene,' Jean told me. 'They offered us huge T-bone steaks at every meal, even breakfast. And the white South Africans were constantly begging to take us out.'

With Kay gone we needed a new head girl, so Sylvia was given the job.

The Tiller name would always draw people in, so theatres up and down the country invited groups of us to go and perform there for summer seasons.

In 1950 Jean, Sylvia, Ruth and I were sent up to a northern seaside town to perform in a summer variety show in a theatre on the sea front. It was the usual list of acts – a tenor, a comedian, an acrobat and a few bands. I enjoyed it because we had to do quite a lot of ballet numbers and had the most amazing costumes thanks to a talented man called Jim. He was the most incredibly skilled dressmaker and made us some beautiful dresses to dance in. My favourite was a pink satin one in which the skirt was made of individually wired pieces of material that overlapped so they looked like rose petals.

'These are for you girls, my beautiful petals,' he said.

'Jim, they're beautiful,' I gasped. 'Come 'ere and give us a kiss.'

He was only young, and was small and dumpy with a round, boyish face. We all knew that he was gay from the minute we saw him prancing around like a queen backstage – even I did, and I was known for my naïvety. In the protective world of the theatre anything goes, and people were allowed to be different and flamboyant; it was just accepted. But if you had put him in the real world in those days, when homosexual acts were illegal, he would have struggled to hide it. Although we didn't know the word for it back then, he was also a transvestite.

'Oh, Irene, I've got a date tonight,' he told me one afternoon as he was measuring us up for a costume. 'Can I borrow your brassiere?'

'Yeah, all right, Jim,' I said, not even batting an eyelid as I stood there in my bra and knickers.

'Do you think I could borrow your tights too, to stuff down my bra?' he said. 'And a squirt of perfume?'

''Course you can, darling,' I said. 'I've got a nice blouse you could try if you wanted?'

We weren't shocked in the slightest. He was such a lovely boy, it didn't matter to us that he wanted to dress up in our underwear and borrow our lipstick. That was just Jim.

'You be careful,' Jean told him. 'You don't want your mother to see you like that.'

He lived with his elderly mother and she didn't have a clue what he did in his private life.

'Ooh, shudder the thought,' he said, 'I think poor Mother would have a heart attack if she saw me all dolled up in my finery.'

Until I met him I never knew that some men liked to do that, and even though I was a bit surprised at first, we just accepted that that's what he did. It didn't bother us and he was such a lovely, talented guy. We felt safe and comfortable with him, and he was no threat to us. We'd be half naked in the dressing-room or he'd measure us for costumes, and we didn't care one bit that he was around.

Sunday was our one day off, and if I knew Mum was at home then I would always try to phone her from our lodgings. One weekend when I was halfway through the summer season I rang, and Mum told me she was between jobs and at a bit of a loose end.

'I know,' I said. 'Why don't you come up here and see me perform?'

Mum didn't sound too keen on the idea.

'Oh, you know, end-of-pier shows are a bit twee for me,' she said. 'They're not really my thing, Rene, and Harry wouldn't like me being away for long.'

'It's not the end of the pier,' I told her. 'It's a small theatre on the sea front. Oh, go on,' I said. 'I'd really love you to come, even if it's just for a couple of nights. You've never seen me dance before and Harry will just have to cope.'

She'd never come to the Palladium like Raymond or been to see any of my shows. When I was child it was because she was abroad during the war, and then later on it was normally because she was working or away on tour. But now that she had some time off there was no excuse.

'All right then,' she said. 'It will be nice to see you.'

I was so excited that after all this time Mum would finally get to watch me dance. But when I went to meet her at the train station I could see that she was like a duck out of water. She was completely out of her comfort zone in a northern seaside town.

'I'm certainly not a snob,' she told me. 'But variety theatres and those sort of acts are all alien to me.'

Her world was classical music and the orchestra pits of London theatres and Sadler's Wells.

I was uncharacteristically nervous as I got ready for that night's performance. I wanted to do my best, as it meant so much to me that Mum was out there watching me dance for the first time.

'I hope she's enjoying it,' I said to Peggy as I peeped out of the curtain during the interval. 'Variety shows aren't really her thing.'

'I bet she's just happy to see you,' she said.

Mum came backstage after the performance, and I introduced her to all the girls and to Jim.

'Well, what did you think?' I asked her.

'I really liked the tenor,' she said. 'He had a wonderful voice and your costumes were lovely. You looked so pretty, Rene.'

'Thank you, Mum,' I said.

But she never said a word about my performance. Secretly I would have loved her to say how wonderful it was or how well she thought that I'd danced, but she didn't say anything.

'Well?' Jean asked me later. 'What did your mum think of your dancing?'

'I honestly don't know,' I told her. 'She didn't say.'

'That's a bit strange,' said Jean.

'Not really,' I replied. 'That's just what she's like. It's not deliberate, she just doesn't have a clue about dancing.'

I knew that if I'd been playing a musical instrument it would have been a different matter, but dancing wasn't really Mum's cup of tea.

My philosophy in life was always never to expect anything, then I wouldn't be disappointed. I'd never had that praise as a child, so in a way I didn't miss it. Although I'd always felt very loved by her, I knew my mother wasn't very good at expressing herself.

Mum stayed the night at our guesthouse, although we didn't share a room as Jean and I were in together. But we got up early and went for a walk.

'Come on then, Rene. Show me the sights,' she said.

We walked down to the sea front, but unfortunately there was a sea fret that was hanging over the beach and you couldn't see a thing for the mist.

'Oh dear, I don't think there's much for us to see,' laughed Mum.

'It's always like this,' I grumbled. 'That mist comes down every morning, clears off for a bit, then it'll be the same by tea-time.'

I wasn't keen on the place, to be honest. In other seaside towns there was always lots to do, but here all we could do was go for a cup of tea or wander down the sea front in the mist.

'I think I'd miss London too much if I was up here,' said Mum, as we walked along arm in arm. 'It's too slow for me. I like to be surrounded by people and be able to jump on the Tube or the buses. And the theatres, of course. No, I'm definitely a city girl,' she sighed.

She came to the show again that night, to be polite, I think, and the next day I walked her back to the station.

'It's gone so fast,' I said, giving her a hug and a kiss. 'Thank you for coming.'

'Well, I'd better get back before Harry starts grumbling,' she said. 'It's been lovely seeing you, Rene.'

I had been so pleased to see her and I felt sad, standing there waving as her train set off for London. She never said it, but I really hoped in my heart that I'd made her proud by all the things I was doing.

I got used to being on the road. I was only home for a few weeks before the whole troupe was sent up to Scotland for a fortnight to perform with Dorothy Lamour, who was appearing at the Glasgow Empire. This was a huge theatre on Sauchiehall Street and we were staying in a boarding house on the same road. We were all a bit nervous about the trip.

'Glasgow's got a reputation for being a bit rough round the edges,' said Sylvia. 'We'd better keep our wits about us, girls.'

Sauchiehall Street itself was a huge, long street that was quite run down in parts and was known for its poverty, violence and crime. All the buildings were grimy and black, and everywhere seemed so dark and dirty. At night a thick smog descended over the whole city.

On our first night after the show we came out of the theatre door and we could only see a few yards in front of us.

'Now link arms, girls,' said Sylvia. 'Let's all stick together and we'll be fine.'

'This reminds me of my summer season,' I joked.

But we were all so terrified that we practically ran down the road to our lodgings, although nothing ever happened to alarm us.

We'd been there a few days when we all trouped out of the stage door one night and there was a small blond man waiting outside. He didn't say anything as we all filed past him, but when I went by he gave me a smile and a wave.

'Looks like you've got yourself a fan there, Irene,' giggled Sylvia.

'Give over,' I said.

But the same fella was there the next night and the next, just hanging around the stage door. Finally on the fourth night when I went past he stepped forward nervously and cleared his throat.

'Excuse me, Miss,' he said in a soft Scottish lilt. 'I've been to the show every night this week and I've waited outside for hours just to get a glimpse of you.'

'Have you really?' I said suspiciously.

'You captivated me from the minute you stepped on stage,' he told me. 'Would you do me the honour of going out with me one evening?'

'What's your name?' I asked.

'It's Gerald,' he said.

'Well, Gerald, that's very kind of you to say that you like my dancing but I'm afraid we're working every night so I won't be able to go out with you. Good night,' I said, wandering off to catch up with the other girls.

He looked disappointed.

'Ooh, I think Irene's got a boyfriend,' teased Jean.

'Don't be silly,' I said. 'I told you, I'm not interested.'

But Gerald was certainly very persistent and he was waiting by the stage door the following night as well.

'Blimey, ticket sales will be through the roof thanks to him,' joked Ruth.

'Hello again,' I said as we all walked past.

'Irene,' he said. 'That is your name, isn't it? Please could I have a word with you?'

'What is it, Gerald?' I sighed. 'I'm tired and I've got to head back to my digs.'

'I'd like to invite you and the rest of the

236

girls to a party at my father's castle,' he said.

'Castle?' I gulped

'Yes,' he said. 'My father's a laird.'

'Oh,' I replied.

'It's on Sunday and if I'm right I think you have the night off.'

'All right then,' I told him. 'You're on. We'll come.'

I was sure the other girls would never forgive me if I passed up an opportunity to go to a party at a real Scottish castle with a laird and lady. I told them what had happened when we got back to our lodgings.

'If I'd known he was aristocracy then I would have chatted him up myself,' said Sylvia.

'It doesn't matter one jot to me,' I said. 'Money and castles don't impress me.'

I liked men who made me laugh, but Gerald seemed a bit dull and oh so serious.

'What on earth are we going to wear to this party?' asked Peggy.

None of us had brought evening dresses with us, so we had to go and hire some. I chose a pink satin strapless number.

'You'll give Gerald palpitations in that,' laughed Jean.

Poor Ruth, though, decided not to go as she wasn't feeling well.

'I think I'll just stay here,' she told us, coughing away. 'I want to make sure that I'm all right for tomorrow's show.'

'You do look a bit pale and wan,' said Sylvia, checking her temperature. 'And you're burning up too.'

'I'll be all right once I get some rest,' she said. 'Have a good time.'

'We'll try,' I smiled.

So the rest of us got taxis out into the countryside to Gerald's family's castle, which couldn't have been more different from the grimy centre of Glasgow.

'Wow,' gasped Jean as we pulled up the gravel driveway.

The place was huge and it was set in magnificent rambling grounds. The castle itself was all lit up and as we walked in there were candles everywhere. All the men were wearing kilts and there were bagpipes playing.

'It's like something out of a film,' said Brenda.

It wasn't long before us girls were invited to join in and we were soon being flung around the dance floor doing the Scottish reel. Gerald soon spotted me.

'There you are, Irene,' he said. 'You look wonderful. Come over here and I'll introduce you to my parents.'

'Only if you're sure,' I said.

'Oh, they're very keen to see you,' he said. 'I've already told them that I've met the girl I want to marry.'

'Pardon?' I said, thinking that I was hearing things.

'I just said that I've told them that I want to marry you,' he repeated.

I was both stunned and terrified.

'But I hardly know you,' I muttered.

That small fact didn't seem to matter to Gerald, and before I could object he led me over to meet his parents. They seemed very nice. I'd never met a lord and lady before, and wasn't sure if I should curtsey.

'Gerald has told us so much about you,' his mother told me. 'He said that you're a wonderful dancer.'

I was just a bit bemused by the whole thing and I didn't know what to say.

'Gerald, I'm very flattered, but you don't know me,' I told him later. 'I live in London. I can't marry you.'

'That doesn't matter to me,' he said.

No matter what I said, he just wouldn't accept that I didn't want to court him, never mind get married.

'What was it like?' croaked Ruth as we all crept in after midnight.

'It was fun,' I whispered. 'We danced the Scottish reel and tried haggis. How are you feeling?'

'Not that great,' she said.

I had hoped that Gerald had got the message by now, so I couldn't believe it when I saw him waiting outside the theatre on our last night. He'd chased me for two whole weeks.

'Hello, Gerald,' I said wearily.

'I know it's your closing night, Irene,' he said. 'So I just wanted to ask you one last time whether you'd consider marrying me?'

'I'm sorry,' I said. 'But I can't.'

'Well, can I come and see you off at the station tomorrow?'

'I really don't think it's a good idea,' I said. 'I'm sorry, Gerald.'

We were at Queen Street station the next day dragging our suitcases onto the train when I saw a figure running down the platform towards us.

'I don't bloomin' believe it,' laughed Peggy. 'Has he still not got the message?'

I panicked and I didn't want him to make a scene.

'Irene!' he shouted. 'Irene!'

'Oh, heck,' I said. 'Tell him I've gone already.'

I jumped into the carriage and locked myself into the toilet. It was the only place I could think of to hide to stop him from seeing me. I could hear Gerald walking up and down the train calling for me.

'Irene,' he yelled. 'Where are you? I've come to say goodbye.'

I was in there ten minutes.

'Come on, set off,' I said to the train, urging it to leave.

At last I heard the guard blow his whistle and the train started moving. As I opened the toilet door I saw a disgruntled Gerald opening the carriage door and jumping out onto the platform.

When he saw me his face lit up.

'Irene,' he shouted, running alongside the carriage. 'Marry me, Irene.'

'Bye, Gerald,' I said, waving through the window.

All the other girls thought it was hilarious.

'Blimey, he was keen,' said Jean.

'He pestered me something chronic,' I said. 'I suppose with all that money he's used to women falling at his feet.'

It was a relief that I was finally shot of him. I wasn't impressed by looks or money. I liked intelligence and someone who made me laugh, and Gerald had just come across as desperate.

'What if he turns up in London?' said Ruth, who seemed to be getting more pale as each day went by.

'Please don't,' I said. 'He wouldn't, would he?'

When we started rehearsing back at the Palladium the following week I was half worried that Gerald would be there by the stage door waiting for me; but thankfully the coast was clear.

However, when I walked into the dressing-room I could tell by the sombre mood that there was something wrong.

'What is it?' I asked. 'What's happened?'

'It's Ruth,' said Peggy, dabbing her eyes with a hanky. 'She's come down with TB, Irene.'

'Oh no,' I gasped.

It was a huge shock. We all knew that she'd been unwell while we'd been up in Glasgow, and she'd been very thin and pale, but none of us had imagined it was that serious.

'Miss Barbara said that the day we got back from Scotland she'd collapsed and had to be rushed to hospital,' Jean told me.

She'd been sent to an isolation ward in a London hospital, so none of us could even go and visit her. It was all very sad, and the thought of TB always made me shudder.

'My father died from TB,' I told the others. 'He literally coughed up blood. At least they've got antibiotics to treat it now.'

When my father had it the most they could do was try to keep you comfortable, or if you were wealthy you were sent off to a sanatorium for a few months in Switzerland where it was hoped the mountain air would aid your recovery.

It was a horrible disease and we were all so upset that sweet little Ruth had got it.

'It's so sad,' sighed Peggy. 'She's such a nice girl.'

'I hope she'll be OK,' I said.

It was very infectious, so we were lucky that the rest of us didn't come down with it. Sadly we never found out what happened to Ruth.

We had no way of contacting her, as we didn't know where her family lived in the Midlands, and Miss Barbara and Miss Doris didn't have a phone number for them. None of us Tillers ever heard from her again. I always wonder about her, and hope that she got better and is alive and well somewhere today.

14

War Wounds

As our train pulled up into Dortmund station we could see the line of photographers waiting on the platform. Their flash bulbs popped away as we stepped out of the carriage.

'*Willkommen*, Tiller Girls,' said the tubby theatre manager who had come to greet us.

He went along the line handing each of us a red rose.

'*Willkommen in Deutschland*,' he said to me, shaking my hand.

'What the heck is he saying?' I whispered to Peggy.

'I'm sorry, Sir,' said Sylvia, our head girl. 'I'm afraid none of us speaks a word of German.'

'Ah, my apologies,' he said in his thick

German accent. 'Velcome to our country, Tiller Girls.'

We grinned for the photographers, who all had huge cameras with big flashbulbs on sticks that nearly blinded us. They got us to pose on the station steps while they clicked away.

'*Tanz!*' one of them shouted.

'*Ja, tanz!*' yelled another one.

We looked quizzically at the theatre manager to see if he could translate and tell us what they wanted.

'Zay are asking you to do ze dance,' he said.

'Oh, I see,' said Peggy.

We linked our arms around each other's backs and did a little kicking routine on the station steps. Afterwards they all broke out into a round of polite applause.

'Vunderful girls,' said the theatre manager. 'Ve Germans love ze Tiller Girls.'

It was November 1950 and we were doing a three-week tour of West Germany, starting in Dortmund, moving on to Düsseldorf and finishing up in a little town called Wuppertal Elberfeld. We'd been invited over there by the theatre managers to star in a variety show and we were performing for a week in each town.

'This is a hugely important visit, girls, and a great honour,' Miss Doris had told us. 'You're the first English dance troupe to perform in Germany since the war.'

We were all nervous, and to be honest I was still a bit scarred from my first brief visit to Germany with the Bluebells. Although it was five years since the war ended, in many people's eyes our countries were still sworn enemies and we weren't sure of the reaction we were going to get from ordinary citizens.

The theatre management had arranged for us all to be put up by local people in their homes. Jean and I were taken off to our digs, which were with a stern-faced, middle-aged couple. As they showed us in they seemed very on edge, which I suspected was because we were English.

'Hello,' said Jean in a very slow, loud voice in the hope that they'd understand. 'Thank you for having us.'

They nodded and smiled back at us nervously.

'Sorry, they don't speak any English,' said the man from the theatre.

'Well, we don't speak any German,' was my reply. 'I'm sure we'll all get by with a bit of nodding and pointing.'

Jean and I decided to go for a walk and explore the town. Dortmund itself was very industrial-looking. The weather was freezing cold, and everything seemed very grey and bleak.

'After the war ended the theatres were one

245

of the first things that the Germans built back up,' Miss Barbara had told us before we'd left.

They wanted to help boost the morale of the country after the war, and they hoped that by featuring big names like us it would help encourage ordinary people back to the theatre and give them something nice to take their minds off the hardships of their daily lives. The one in Dortmund had been badly damaged by bombing but had been completely refurbished, and everything was sparkling and new – totally different from the historic Palladium.

It was strange walking around the town. Any money had obviously been poured into getting businesses going, so there were all these gleaming new shops and cafés. But as we went further down the same road we got a shock when we saw the houses in which ordinary Germans lived.

'Blimey, what a mess,' I gasped, as we saw street after street of bombed-out houses that hadn't been rebuilt after the war.

We were horrified to see that there were families living in these dilapidated buildings that didn't have electricity or running water.

'Look at that place,' said Jean.

An explosion had ripped off the whole side of one house so it was opened up like a doll's house. What used to be a children's bedroom was now exposed to the elements, the wallpaper flapping in the wind. There was a makeshift roof, and although some of the windows had been boarded up, through a downstairs one we could see a family cooking their dinner over a fire built in a hole in the ground.

'The poor things must be freezing,' I said.

I couldn't believe there were so many people living in these terrible conditions. You had these beautiful brand new shops and cafés serving gorgeous gâteaux and frothy hot chocolate, but in the same street you had families living in bombed-out houses, struggling to feed themselves.

'It makes you realise how the war has affected everyone,' I sighed.

It certainly showed us the other side of the war, and it was a total contrast to the opulence that I'd experienced in the American nightclub in the Alps with the Bluebells.

'I feel awful for celebrating now,' said Jean. 'Look what we did to these poor people.'

Back home people had cheered and chanted 'Down with Germany' when they'd heard on the radio that multiple German cities and towns had been successfully bombed. But seeing their country for myself with my own eyes made me realise that they were just like us. Most Germans were ordinary people trying to make the best of their lives after the devastation of the war.

'I can see that my father and my brother

247

were right,' I said. 'There are no winners when it comes to war.'

Both of our countries had suffered, millions of people had lost their lives, and whole towns and cities had been reduced to rubble by the bombing.

'Sometimes war feels completely pointless,' agreed Jean.

We were all a bit worried about how our appearance at the theatre was going to go down with the German audience. It felt very odd being top of the bill as we weren't used to that. There was a whole list of weird and wonderful supporting acts that would be performing with us every night. They included a contortionist and a comedian, though obviously we didn't understand a word of his routine because it was in German. At rehearsals one day we saw a rather odd-looking woman with long, flowing grey hair clutching a violin.

'She looks a bit strange,' whispered Peggy as she came shuffling on stage. 'I wonder what she does.'

It turned out that she was a tightrope walker, and while she did it she would play these dreadful songs. But none of us could believe our eyes when we realised that her violin was electric and lit up while she performed. It was absolutely horrendous and we all had to stop ourselves from laughing.

'My poor mother would have a fit if she

248

saw this,' I said.

The standard of performance was really terrible compared with the people we worked with back at home. This was because the British entertainment industry had carried on during the war, many theatres had stayed open and people had joined ENSA, whereas in Germany the whole entertainment industry had been shut down for years.

Much to our relief, the show was sold out every night and we got a great reaction from the crowd.

'Thank goodness they're clapping,' I smiled as we took a bow.

While we were there we were also invited to go and visit the British Military Hospital in Münster.

'The press will come and take some photographs but you won't be expected to put on a performance,' Miss Barbara had told us before we left.

We weren't sure what we were there to do, really.

'I think it's just to look pretty for the cameras, flutter your eyelashes at the injured soldiers and help boost morale,' said Sylvia.

We didn't go in costumes or wear our Tiller uniforms but we all wore nice dresses, winter coats and hats, and a full face of make-up. When we walked into the ward all of the soldiers were lying in bed, grinning from ear to ear when they saw us.

'They don't look that injured,' I whispered to Sylvia. 'What do you think they're in for?'

'I've no idea,' she said. 'I get the feeling this is just a good PR exercise for the Tillers and the Palladium.'

The photographers snapped away as we walked up and down the ward chatting to the soldiers. I went and sat with one man who had his leg in a cast and raised up on a pulley.

''Ello, luv,' he said in a broad Yorkshire accent. 'I 'aven't seen a lovely lass like you in months.'

'Oh, well, it's your lucky day then,' I told him. 'How did you hurt your leg?'

I could tell he was a bit embarrassed about it.

'It's nowt dramatic,' he said. 'I were kicking a football round with some German lads and took a tumble. Not right heroic, I know, but it bloody well hurt, I tell thee.'

'Well, I hope you get better soon,' I said.

'Thank you, dear,' he said. 'A visit from you has cheered me up no end. Me wife will be spitting feathers when she finds out I've been chatted up by one of them Tiller Girls. Now 'old onto yer 'at when you go out, lass, as I bet it's a bit parky out there.'

'I will do,' I said. 'Now you take care of yourself.'

He was a nice man and I was pleased to

have given him a bit of cheer in that dreary place.

A week later it was on to Düsseldorf, which was a much prettier town. The theatre we were performing in had been destroyed in the war so it had all been completely rebuilt. It was beautiful, with amazing lighting, and it was all very swish.

This time the woman whom Jean and I were lodging with spoke some English, so at least we could chat to her.

'Thank you for putting us up,' I said. 'I know it must be strange having English people to stay.'

'You British are not a threat to us any more,' she said. 'Like you, we're just glad that the war is over.'

She described how many ordinary people were in the dark about what was happening in their own country.

'We didn't know that concentration camps existed, let alone what was going on in them,' she told us.

But not every German was as friendly or welcomed us with open arms. One day Peggy, Jean and I went for a walk around the town centre before the show. We were laughing and chatting away as we walked down the street when an old man came over to us.

'*Drecksau*,' he scowled.

'I'm sorry, Sir, we don't speak any German,' Peggy politely told him, but he turned out to be a bit of a linguist.

'Bloody English pigs,' he sneered, spitting at us before walking off.

We were all so shocked that we just stood there stunned in the middle of the street. We were terrified and I was shaking. None of us dared say anything back to him.

'Well, he was a rather unpleasant man,' said Peggy.

'Come on, girls,' said Jean, and we all linked arms and hurried back to the safety of the theatre.

The other girls were appalled when we told them that we'd been sworn at and spat on in the street.

'I suppose to some German people we English will always be their enemy,' said Sylvia.

The poverty in these cities was also a big surprise to us all. One afternoon we were walking to the theatre when I saw an ex-serviceman sitting in the gutter holding out his hand to us. His uniform was all tatty and threadbare, and he had a tray around his neck filled with boxes of matches.

'Oh, my goodness,' I whispered to Brenda.

'What is it, Irene?' she said.

'Look, that poor man has got no eyes,' I told her.

He didn't have any eyeballs and both eyes were literally empty sockets. It was so shocking.

He must have heard our high heels clopping on the cobbles because as we walked past he reached out his hand towards us.

'*Streichhölzer!*' he cried, which I assumed was the German word for matches.

This horrified us all and we didn't know what to do, so we just hurried past. It was ghastly to see someone so badly injured, but sadly it became a common occurrence to see blind ex-servicemen begging or selling matches in the street.

Throughout the whole of our trip the one place where we always felt safe was in the theatres. That's the peculiar thing about show business. It doesn't matter where anyone comes from or what their beliefs are or what language they speak, you're all united by the show. Once you walk through that theatre door you all come together as a team. The German theatre managers made a big fuss of us and they seemed very chuffed to have got us over there. It was another step towards getting things back to normal after the war and to encourage people into the theatres again.

Finally we moved on to Wuppertal, which was a very pretty little town. Jean and I were sent to stay with an elderly couple. The house was immaculately clean and tidy, and we had a huge bedroom that was all white and pristine. That night after rehearsals Jean and I sat in our big bed smoking.

'What do you think this is?' she said, inspecting the big, white, fluffy quilt on our bed. 'Where are the sheets and blankets?'

'I think it's what you call a duvet,' I said. 'I've heard about them before. They've got lots of feathers stuffed inside them.'

'How very continental,' said Jean, taking a big drag on her cigarette.

But to our horror, a bit of burning ash dropped off the end and landed on the duvet. Before we knew it, it was smouldering.

We both panicked, but thankfully Jean managed to waft it out.

'Oh, sugar,' she yelled. 'It's only gone and burned a hole in the bloomin' thing.'

We'd only been there a couple of hours and already we were managing to wreck the place. We were dreading telling our hosts what we'd done the next morning.

'I'm so sorry,' said Jean, showing them the damage to their pristine white duvet. 'I managed to burn a hole in it last night.'

The woman tutted loudly and shook her head. Then she showed it to her husband, who looked stern. He wagged his finger at us and said something in German that we didn't understand.

'I don't think they're very happy,' I whispered to Jean.

'I'm ever so sorry,' she told them again.

Funnily enough neither of us dared smoke in bed again.

Finally our three-week tour was over and in a way it was a relief to get home.

'How was it?' asked my mother. 'Did you enjoy yourself?'

'I wouldn't say that,' I told her. 'But it was definitely an experience.'

It really had been an education for us and opened our eyes to the harsh reality of what was happening abroad. It had certainly brought it home to me that post-war Germany was a shattered nation desperately trying to get itself back on its feet. And we were about to see for ourselves how the war had devastated some of our own men.

15

Horror and High Tea

Pandemonium was the only word to describe the scene in the dressing-room at the London Palladium as twenty giggling girls squeezed themselves into identical white cowgirl outfits.

It was a Sunday afternoon in April 1950. We didn't normally work on Sundays – in fact it was usually our only day off – but today was different. As the top troupe of Tiller Girls in the country we had been invited to dance at a charity concert to raise money for airmen and soldiers who had been seriously injured in the war.

It was being held in the ballroom of the glitzy five-star Grosvenor hotel in Mayfair. We were all in a flap as we weren't just performing our high-kicking cowgirl routine for the wounded servicemen; we had been told that there would be a specially invited audience of wealthy businessmen there as well.

'I'll bet there'll be some oil barons,' said Peggy, as she pulled on her white tasselled bolero jacket. 'The place will be crawling with rich people.'

'Ooh, just think, we might get swept off our feet by a millionaire,' said Sylvia.

'Don't hold your breath,' I laughed. 'Now pass me the hot black.'

Crowding around the mirrors, we expertly blobbed it onto the end of each eyelash, painted on our trademark scarlet lipstick and rubbed our cheeks with carmine.

Soon we were all ready to go in our white shirts and tasselled jackets, high-cut white shorts, white gloves and white Stetsons. We clattered down the steep stone staircase from our dressing-room right at the top of the theatre to find a fleet of black limousines waiting outside.

'This is the life,' sighed Sylvia. 'I could definitely get used to this.'

We were all thrilled about being invited to a posh hotel like the Grosvenor, and our excitement had reached fever pitch by the time we pulled up outside the imposing Victorian building on Park Lane. I couldn't believe it when a man in a smart navy uniform stepped forward to open the car door and another held open the large front doors for us. I felt like one of the dignitaries arriving for a Royal Command Performance.

As we walked into the grand entrance we all ooh'd and aah'd. The whole place exuded elegance and luxury, from the gold staircase and the plush red carpet to the ornately painted ceiling, where the biggest crystal chandelier I'd ever seen in my life twinkled in the light.

'Flippin' 'eck,' said Peggy.

'Isn't it beautiful?' I sighed, gawping like a goldfish.

It was certainly a stark contrast to our rundown kitchen at home with its stone sink, and the freezing cold outside toilet where I sat on the loo and watched spiders spin their webs. Life at the Grosvenor was a lot more luxurious.

'I heard it costs more than £50 a night to stay here,' Jean whispered.

'I can see why,' I said.

For the first time in my life I could see what real wealth looked like and it took my breath away. The ballroom was just as grand as the rest of the hotel, but a lot more intimate than the huge Palladium. We were performing alongside Bob Hope, who was over from America for two weeks to do another season at the Palladium.

'I hope he's a bit more friendly this time,' I said. He hardly spoke to anyone when we'd last done a show with him.

Around a hundred businessmen were already there, tucking into dainty sandwiches, and the champagne was flowing. I think we were all a bit disappointed when we saw the middle-aged group in their suits.

'What a dull bunch,' sighed Jean.

'So much for tall, dark, handsome millionaires,' said Sylvia. 'None of this stuffy lot would make my heart race.'

Just then the hotel manager came rushing over to us.

'Ladies, the servicemen have arrived,' he said. 'The ambulances are just pulling up outside.'

All we'd been told was that the men were coming from a hospital in Sussex and there was a mixture of wounded soldiers and airmen who'd been burned when their planes had gone down. We lined up by the entrance ready to flutter our eyelashes and welcome them in. But as the ballroom doors swung open I certainly wasn't prepared for the sight that greeted us.

Two or three men hobbled in on crutches,

while behind them came many others who had lost their legs and were being pushed in wheelchairs by nurses from the Red Cross. Then there were the poor airmen who had been left terribly burned and disfigured. Plastic surgery was still in its infancy then, and some of them didn't have noses or ears and their faces were a mass of jagged scars from all of the skin grafts they'd had. I could tell that a few of them were wearing wigs and had glass eyes.

'Hello, girls,' said one man as he walked past, and as he gave us a wave I could see he'd lost most of the fingers on his badly scarred hand.

I didn't want him to see how shocked I was.

'Welcome to the Grosvenor, Sir,' I said, flashing him a smile. 'I hope you enjoy the show.'

'Oh, I'm sure we will when beauties like you are in it,' he replied.

I couldn't believe what I was seeing, and I could tell from the look on their faces that the other girls were as shocked as I was.

'Oh, my goodness,' whispered Jean, tears pricking her eyes. 'These poor fellas.'

'It's terrible,' mumbled Sylvia. 'I can hardly bear to look at them.'

The servicemen were all dressed in what were known as convalescent blues. This was the uniform all injured war veterans had to

wear so that people would be able to recognise them (and also, it was rumoured, so that
pub landlords would know not to serve them
alcohol!). It consisted of a shapeless blue
flannelette jacket and matching trousers that
looked like a pair of ill-fitting pyjamas.

But no matter how shocked we were, I
knew we couldn't let these men see the horror and the pity we were feeling. I thought
back to what Miss Doris always told us:
'You're here to do a job, and that's to entertain.'

All we could do was stand there with big
grins plastered on our faces as the servicemen were helped to their seats at the front
of the ballroom.

Up until then I hadn't really thought about
why we were there that day, and suddenly I
felt very guilty. Here we were, all silly and
giggly, joking about being asked out by
millionaires, and here were these poor young
men who had been horrifically injured.

Before the show started we were supposed
to serve them afternoon tea, but it just
didn't seem right to me.

'I feel so false,' I said to Sylvia as I put some
fine china cups and saucers onto a tray. 'How
can watching us leaping and prancing about
on stage help them? Being poured a cup of
tea by a Tiller Girl's not going to make much
of a difference to their lives, is it?'

'I know what you mean,' she said. 'But

look how happy they are to see us.'

It was true. Most of the servicemen had big grins on their faces, and on the way in a few of them had even given us a cheeky wink.

'It's a big deal for them,' said Sylvia. 'It's a chance for them to get out of the hospital for once and see some eye candy. I bet the only women they get to see are those po-faced Florence Nightingales over there.'

I realised she was right. Most of these lads had spent the five years since the end of the war in hospital, and I'd heard that often their wives and girlfriends left them because they couldn't cope with the severity of their injuries. It was probably a real treat for them to come to a posh hotel and see a famous dance troupe known for its glamorous girls perform especially for them.

'Let's get them a cuppa, then,' I said.

But before we could start, a Red Cross nurse wearing a stiffly starched white uniform and a cape hat bustled over to us.

'Please be very careful how you speak to the patients,' she said brusquely. 'Do not under any circumstances ask them about their injuries.'

We all nodded politely. I suddenly felt ridiculous, dolled up to the nines in my cowgirl costume. It seemed acceptable in the theatre in front of a paying audience, but here we were up close and personal with these horrifically injured men and it made what we did seem really frivolous somehow.

'I must also warn you about the gentleman that we're about to bring in,' she said. 'Unfortunately he has very severe injuries. He has lost most of his limbs, he's blind and his windpipe was badly burned so he's unable to speak. I think it's probably best if you don't say anything at all to him as we don't want to cause him any upset.'

Before we could even take in what she had said, the most horrifically injured man that I had ever seen in my life was carried into the ballroom on a stretcher. His burns must have been extensive because his whole body was completely covered in bandages except for a small gap for his mouth. He had a blanket over him, but I could see he had no arms and God only knows if he still had his legs. We all tried not to stare at this ruined shell of a man but it was truly shocking.

'What are we going to do about him?' whispered Jean. 'We can't exactly offer him a cup of tea and a biccy.'

'It's a miracle how he's even survived,' I said. 'What kind of quality of life is he going to have in that state?'

I think I went into shock, I was so horrified by how injured these men were. This was a side of the war that I had only glimpsed on our visit to Germany. In Great Britain there had been all the victory parades, the street parties and the heroes being awarded medals. But suddenly here was the reality of war, slapping us right in the face. Young men whose lives had been ruined for ever, their limbs blown off by shrapnel or who had been so badly burned that they no longer had a face. We'd won the war, but so many people had paid a terrible price.

It also seemed so wrong to me having all these millionaires there. Here they were, quaffing champagne and nibbling on dainty sandwiches in their expensive suits, while across the room were these poor, injured men.

While the millionaires tucked into the champagne, we got on with serving after-noon tea to the servicemen. I went over to one gentleman who I could see had lost an arm.

'Would you like a cup of tea and a biscuit?' I asked, and he nodded.

'Thank you,' he said. 'You're the prettiest girl I've seen in a long time. I'm surprised you even want to talk to me. Most women see my stump and run a mile.'

'Well, more fool them,' I told him. 'You seem like a lovely man.'

I went and got his tea and a shortbread, and brought it back to him.

'What are you doing after the show?' he asked me.

'Oh, I've got to go home and get my

263

beauty sleep,' I joked.

'And I'll have to go back to that prison they call a hospital,' he said sadly.

I just felt so desperately sorry for them all.

Once high tea had been served it was show time. We were used to dancing on the huge stage of the Palladium with all the dazzling lights and accompanied by a big band. But today the setting was a lot more intimate and we just had a quartet of musicians provided by the hotel. We were performing on the dance floor of the ballroom, literally a few feet away from the soldiers, with no special lighting, and I felt very exposed and 'on show'. Normally we couldn't see anyone in the audience, but here I could see every single one of their faces and their reactions. It was overwhelming in a different way and it felt more like the cabaret-type atmosphere that I'd experienced briefly with the Blue-bells.

'I don't know where to look,' whispered Peggy.

'Just focus on one or two of them in the front row and just keep smiling,' I told her. 'Let's give them something nice to watch.'

I knew I was going to find it hard too, dancing away with a big grin plastered on my face for these poor injured men. But I was also very aware that this was their big treat and I wanted to do a good job for them.

As the music started and we began our

routine, I relaxed into it. I could see the big grins on the soldiers' faces and those that could were clapping enthusiastically along to the lively jazz number. Dancing had always made me feel happy, and it had been my safe place away from the harsh realities of the outside world, but for the first time I really appreciated the fact that it made others happy too and provided them with an escape.

We finished our high-kicking cowgirl routine to rapturous applause and we even got a few wolf whistles from our grateful audience. I didn't get the same buzz I got from performing in a huge West End theatre, but rather a quiet satisfaction that we'd done a nice performance for these men and provided some much-needed fun, frivolity and eye candy to take their minds briefly off their terrible injuries and the monotony of their lives in hospital.

'Did you see the big grins on their faces?' asked Sylvia. 'They loved it.'

'I think they really enjoyed it,' I said.

It sounds like a real cliché, but performing for them that afternoon really was very humbling. Afterwards it was Bob Hope's turn and he had them all in stitches. It was nice to see them all laughing and enjoying themselves.

I stared at the horrifically injured man lying at the front on the stretcher.

'I wonder what on earth he makes of it all,' I said to Sylvia. 'Do you think he even knows where he is or can hear what's going on?'

What kind of life was he ever going to lead?

'Perhaps it would have been kinder if he'd died in the war,' said Jean, and I knew what she meant.

When the show was over we were each handed a silver tray that looked a bit like a cake-tin lid and we went to chat up the wealthy guests.

'Come on, gentlemen,' I said, flashing them my best smile. 'Put your hands in your pockets. It's all going to help the servicemen.'

'Oh, I'd never say no to a Tiller Girl,' laughed one portly, grey-haired man, giving me a wink and pushing a £50 note into my hand.

Bob Hope was chatting to them and he had them all eating out of his hand.

'Come on, fellas,' he said. 'Let's give these girls something to smile about. They've given up their day off to help the servicemen.'

'It was worth it to meet such distinguished guests as yourself,' I told them, rattling my tray.

Flattery gets you everywhere, and soon my tray was piled high with £50 and £100 notes. I'd never even seen that sort of money before and my eyes were practically popping out of my head.

'Look,' I hissed to Jean, whose tray also had a mountain of cash on it. 'There must be thousands of pounds here.'

Afterwards we all posed on the stairs with Bob Hope for a photograph for the following day's newspapers. The Palladium's management liked us Tillers to be seen doing charitable deeds.

Suddenly the fierce-looking Red Cross nurse clapped her hands loudly to get everyone's attention.

'I'm afraid the fun is over now, gentlemen, and it's time to get back to the hospital,' she told the servicemen, who all groaned and booed.

'I'm going to run away with the Tillers!' a man with one leg in a wheelchair shouted.

'I don't think you'll be doing much running, my friend,' said the airman sat next to him.

We lined up by the door and waved them goodbye as they were helped out into the waiting ambulances. As we were driven back to the Palladium to change, the mood in our car was very different from the one coming. I think we were all shocked and stunned by what we had seen that afternoon. I know I was deeply affected by it, and the sight of those servicemen is something that has stayed with me ever since. Even now, sixty-four years later, when I close my eyes I can still see the image of that poor burned soldier on his stretcher and I often wonder what happened to him.

But that wasn't to be the end of my involvement with servicemen. A few weeks later Miss Doris came to see me in the dressing-room at the Palladium.

'I've got some good news for you, Irene,' she said. 'Some editors from *Blighty* magazine came to see the show last night and they picked you out of the whole troupe. They want to know if you'd be willing to pose for their pin-up-girl pages.'

'Oh,' I said, shocked. 'I'm not sure I'm really pin-up material.'

Blighty described itself as a weekly humorous magazine for British servicemen containing pin-up pictures, cartoons and stories. The women in it were always fully clothed, and as far as I was concerned it was all above board and nothing seedy. It had been set up and distributed to boost the morale of lonely soldiers during the Second World War, and the pin-up pictures were the most popular section. Servicemen would pin them up in their lockers, on the walls of their barracks and even on the sides of planes.

'We'll have to get permission from the Palladium management, of course, but that shouldn't be a problem,' said Miss Doris.

She explained that I would have to go to a London studio for a photo shoot and I would be paid two guineas for my time.

The other Tillers thought it was a hoot, and I was relieved that they didn't seem in the slightest bit jealous.

'Oh, look, here comes Marilyn Monroe,' joked Peggy the next day when I walked into the dressing-room.

'You won't want to know us when you hit the big time,' said Jean.

'Don't be silly,' I said. 'It's just a silly photo to give the servicemen a bit of cheer.'

Pin-up poses were very fashionable at the time and several Hollywood stars like Ava Gardner and Rita Hayworth had posed for this style of photograph. The girls thought it was hilarious that I would be adorning lockers of lonely servicemen around the world. I'd done a bit of modelling for knitting patterns while I was at Italia Conti, but nothing as glamorous as this.

On the day of the shoot I was a bag of nerves as I headed to the photographer's studio just off Oxford Street. I didn't know what to expect, but I'd been told to bring my own underwear and shoes. I stood there awkwardly in my plain black bra and high-waisted pants, fishnet tights and black, high-heeled Mary Jane's while the photographer warmed up his Box Brownie camera and placed it on a tripod. He was a tubby, balding man in his fifties but he seemed nice enough. He came over to me, moved me side on and made me rest a bended knee on a little table, then handed me a powder puff with a long, wooden handle.

'That's it, dear, big smiles,' he said, snapping away. 'Pretend you've just got out of the tub and you're using the puff to put talcum powder on your back.'

I felt a bit silly at first, but after five minutes I soon got into the swing of things. I then sat at a dressing table and posed for several more shots, clutching a string of pearls in my cupped hands.

'Stunning,' said the photographer. 'Those soldiers will think it's Christmas when they see a long-legged lovely like you.'

One month later I made my debut in the 'Pin-Up Parade' section of the magazine.

A few weeks later Val Parnell came to see me in the dressing-room. I was quaking in my boots when I saw that the big boss of the theatre was waiting for me.

'Miss Starr?' he said.

'Yes, Sir,' I nodded, terrified I was going to get my marching orders.

'I think someone's got themselves a bit of a fan club,' he smiled, handing me a big bundle of letters.

Puzzled, I flicked through them. They were all addressed to 'Irene Starr, Pin-up girl c/o The London Palladium' and they were covered with all kinds of exotic-looking foreign stamps.

'It must be some of the lonely servicemen

who saw you in *Blighty*,' laughed Brenda.

'Go on, Irene. Open them,' said Sylvia.

'Blimey, this one's stamped as being from a naval ship called HMS *Ceylon* in Bahrain,' I said.

I ripped it open and read it aloud.

Dear Miss Starr,

I'm not at all certain that this letter will reach you. All I can do is hope and put my trust in the GPO that they will find you. I saw your photo in an issue of Blighty. Wow! I could describe my feelings and dwell on your beauty but there aren't enough pieces of paper in the canteen to enable me to expand on your charms.

It was a smashing pose and, looking at the photo, I can see why the page was called 'Pin-Up Parade'. It now adorns my locker door and makes opening it a little bit more worthwhile.

Keep the show going until December 1951 and I will be there. I was going to ask if you wanted a penpal but I'm sure that's out of the question.

Wishing you all the best.

Yours faithfully,

Victor

All the girls were in fits by the time I'd finished.

'Well, Victor's certainly soft on you,' said Sylvia. 'You must write back to him.'

'I'll do no such thing,' I said. 'I don't want to encourage him.'

Another letter was stamped as being from an RAF hospital in Wiltshire.

Dear Miss Starr,

In December of last year I was in a bazaar in Faluja, a small town 32 miles from Baghdad in Iraq when I went into a little shop and saw a photo of you pinned up on the wall. Underneath the caption it said that you were in a show at the London Palladium. I was determined to come and find you and see the show but when I arrived back in the UK I was in an accident and ended up in hospital where I will be for some time. I would love to meet you and I would like to hear back from you if you had a few moments to spare.

Yours sincerely,
Flying Officer Simpson

'Oh, poor Officer Simpson,' said Jean. 'I wonder how he got injured?'

I was just stunned that my photograph had turned up in a market thousands of miles away near Baghdad. As I read all of the other fan letters I just felt so sorry for all these servicemen. Like the injured soldiers and airmen that we'd danced for, they hardly had any female contact and it was such a big deal for them to see these pin-up pictures. It certainly was a lonely sort of a life being in the forces. But unlike most of the other Tillers, I wasn't interested in men

272

and didn't think they were worth the hassle. As some of the other girls were about to find out, they often meant trouble.

16

Man Trouble

The one topic of conversation that came up most frequently in our dressing-room at the Palladium was men. Whether it was who was going out with whom, who'd broken up with whom or who was getting married, there was always some gossip or drama going on when it came to matters of the opposite sex.

One day a member of the troupe, a girl called Brenda, came into the dressing-room in floods of tears.

'What is it?' I asked her. 'You look awful. Come and sit down and tell me what's happened.'

She looked so shaken up that I thought someone close to her must have died.

'Oh, Irene,' she sobbed. 'It's Fred. He's finished with me.'

Fred was the older man who she had been seeing for the past six months. None of us had met him but we knew she was totally besotted.

'You see, the thing was, he was married,' she said. 'He promised me that he'd leave his wife but he phoned me today and told me that's it all over, just like that.'

'Oh, Brenda,' I sighed. 'Why didn't you tell us that he was a married man?'

'Because I was ashamed,' she said, snivelling into her handkerchief. 'I didn't want you all to think bad of me.'

'You know we wouldn't do that,' I told her. 'But honestly it sounds like you're better off without him. What a pig.'

'Irene's right,' said Peggy. 'It sounds like he was leading you a merry dance.'

We were all such a close-knit group and we had few secrets from each other. We spent so much time together in the theatre, but once we left through that stage door at night we all went off in different directions. We didn't see what anyone's home life was like, and often that meant that we'd tell each other more than we would our families or close friends who didn't work in the industry.

'Dry your eyes,' said Sylvia, passing Brenda a tissue. 'It's time to get ready for tonight's show and you can't go on stage with your face all puffy like that.'

But she was still weeping buckets.

'Oh, Sylvia, you won't tell Miss Barbara and Miss Doris, will you?' she cried. 'They'd have a fit if they knew I was seeing a married man.'

'Of course I won't,' she said. 'I won't mention a word.'

Miss Barbara and Miss Doris still kept a watchful eye over us from a distance and Sylvia had to report back to them every week. If there were any new boyfriends on the scene, then she was supposed to inform them as they liked to meet potential suitors to check that they were good enough for one of their girls. So if anyone was seeing a bit of a rogue or someone who might be classed as unsuitable then they'd keep it quiet or beg Sylvia not to say anything.

They were always quick to remind us that it was our responsibility to keep up the respectable, straight-laced image that the Tiller Girls were supposed to project.

'We're not all feathers and bras here like the Bluebell Girls,' said Miss Doris. 'Tillers are seen as the girls next door.'

Going out with a married man certainly wouldn't fit in with their idea of good behaviour, so we were all careful to keep that one quiet.

For some unknown reason I became the mother hen of our dressing-room at the Palladium. All the girls seemed to come to me if they needed a confidante or wanted advice, even when it concerned men.

'Go ask Irene, she'll tell you what to do,' became the standard response if someone had a problem.

Even though I was one of the younger girls, in a way I seemed older than my years. It was partly down to the fact that I'd brought myself up to a certain extent, while many of the girls had been mollycoddled by their parents. I think they also came to me because they knew I would never be judgemental – it just wasn't in my nature. My grandparents and my mum's siblings had judged me, and I knew how much that hurt, so I would never criticise anyone. But when it came to men, I really didn't have a clue.

'I don't know why you all ask me,' I said. 'I know nothing about men. I haven't even got a boyfriend.'

I was adamant I didn't want one either. The girls all teased me because I was steadfastly single.

'When are you going to get yourself a fella, Irene?' Jean asked me one day. 'Is there no one that's caught your eye?'

'Honestly, I'm not interested,' I told her. 'I don't know why you're all so obsessed about it, especially when I hear you lot complaining about your blokes and how awfully they treat you.'

Men were an alien species to me and I had no experience of adult relationships. I never saw my grandparents being affectionate with each other and I'd grown up without a father in my life.

'Listening to all your wretched stories, I

don't think I want a boyfriend,' I told them.

As far as I saw it, you had to be all excited about having a boyfriend, and that was some girls' main aim in life. You were always made to feel you were a failure if you didn't have one, and I couldn't understand why. I just didn't feel like that.

As far as I could see, boys were nothing but trouble. In the early Fifties every young, unmarried woman lived in fear of getting pregnant and over the years there were a few scares in our dressing-room.

I'll never forget the day Jean came into work looking ashen-faced.

'You all right, Jean?' I asked.

'Yes,' she said, but I could hear the wobble in her voice and she promptly burst into tears.

'Oh, Irene,' she whispered. 'I'm late.'

'What do you mean late?' I asked, naïve as usual.

'I mean my monthlies are late,' she said.

My face fell and suddenly I knew exactly what she meant.

'Oh, God, Irene, what if I'm pregnant?' she sobbed. 'My parents will want nothing more to do with me. They'll probably send me to one of those homes where you're forced to give up your baby and have it adopted.'

I didn't know what to say. In those days getting pregnant was every girl's biggest fear. The Pill hadn't yet been invented and there was no real contraception for women. As an unmarried woman there was no way on this earth you would be able to go to the doctor and ask about birth control. Young girls got desperate, and we'd all heard horrendous stories about backstreet abortions in London. It made my hair stand on end just thinking about it.

'Well, if you are pregnant, won't Kenneth do the right thing and marry you?' I said.

Jean just shrugged.

'He might not want anything more to do with me,' she said, biting her lip to try to hold back the tears in front of the other girls.

'I'm so ashamed I've even got myself into this predicament,' she sighed. 'How could I have been so stupid?'

There was nothing I could do to make her feel better. If she was pregnant we both knew that that would be the end of her career as a Tiller Girl and she would probably be ostracised by her family and sent to live somewhere else in disgrace.

There were no home pregnancy tests then, so the only way of knowing for sure was by missing periods.

'What about your doctor?' I said. 'Can you go and see him?'

'I can't,' she sobbed. 'I know he'll just go and tell my parents.'

Poor Jean, I felt so sorry for her having that preying on her mind. But a week later she pulled me to one side.

'Thank God, I'm on the rag after all,' she said. 'My system must be all messed up for some reason.'

'Oh, Jean, I'm so relieved for you,' I said.

It made me even more sure that I didn't want a boyfriend and all the complications that came with it.

In any case there wasn't much time to meet anyone outside our own little world. We worked six evenings a week and after the show we'd all run for the last Tube home. As Tiller Girls, we were never short of male attention, though. There were always plenty of male fans waiting outside the stage door for us. We even had our very own stalker – a young man called George, who used to follow us around the country. We first noticed him standing outside the Palladium.

'Please can I have your autographs, girls?' he asked one night as we all came dashing out after a performance.

'Well, you seem like a nice presentable young man, so I'm sure we can do that for you,' said Peggy.

'My name's George,' he told us, and we all signed his book.

But a few weeks later we were performing a one-off show in Manchester and can you guess who was waiting by the stage door when we came out afterwards?

'Isn't that the same fellow who was at the

Palladium last week?' asked Sylvia.

He was very memorable because he had a shock of curly red hair. He couldn't have been any more than twenty, and he was very quiet and polite.

'Hello,' I said. 'Fancy seeing you again. What are you doing in Manchester?'

'I just love you Tiller Girls,' he told us, blushing. 'I'm your number one fan and I come to as many shows as I can.'

'Well, if that's how you want to spend your time and money that's fine by us,' said Sylvia.

'He seems harmless enough,' I whispered to Jean.

We all thought it was quite sweet and funny, and there was nothing creepy about him. From then on, wherever we went in the country from Scotland to Portsmouth, George would often pop up outside the stage door, and he'd be outside the Palladium at least once a week.

'All right, George,' we would call when we all came out, and we'd give him a friendly pat on the head as you would to a pet dog.

'I know,' I said one day. 'George can be our mascot.'

When we suggested it to him that night he seemed very chuffed that he was the unofficial mascot of the Tillers' top troupe.

'It's an incredible honour, girls,' he told us seriously. 'Thank you so much.'

Inside the theatre we were always getting chatted up too. It came with the job, really. When we first started, Miss Barbara and Miss Doris had warned us about coping with unwanted advances.

'Keep away from the comedians and the compères, girls,' they had told us. 'They're notorious for their wandering hands.'

They had been right too. They didn't mean the big stars, just the ordinary, run-of-the-mill support acts who made a living from performing in variety shows.

But we just learned to take everything with a pinch of salt and brush off any innuendos. There were a couple of middle-aged comedians who had a particularly bad reputation for this, and Brenda had a run-in with one of them.

'The cheeky beggar gave my bum a pat yesterday when I passed him in the wings,' she said. 'Then today he tried to shove his hand down my bra at rehearsals.'

'Did you say anything?' I asked.

'Oh, no,' she said. 'I just gave him a slap round the chops and that seemed to do the trick. He's not tried anything since.'

In those days wandering hands were seen as part of the job and you just learned not to take offence.

The Skyrockets always enjoyed flirting with us chorus girls too. They were mainly older men, and most of them had wives and children, but they couldn't resist a bit of banter. I caught the eye of one of them called Bert who would always make a beeline for me during rehearsals. He was a jolly, happy bloke, as well as a fine musician, and I liked him.

'Hello, Irene,' he'd say with a big grin on his face. 'How's my favourite girl today?'

'Oh, give over, Bert,' I'd reply, rolling my eyes.

We'd chat about music, and he was impressed by how much I knew because my mother was a professional musician.

'I think you're lovely,' he told me one day. 'Would you like to come fishing with me one morning?'

'Fishing?' I laughed. 'You must be joking.'

'Yes,' he said. 'I get up and go out most mornings around 6 a.m. You can catch all sorts, you know.'

'No thanks, Bert,' I said. 'There's no way I'm getting up that early and I don't like fishing.'

I also had another admirer at the Palladium. Arthur was a middle-aged bachelor, and even though he was single I didn't find him in the least bit attractive. He was a portly little man and he always wore the same old shabby suit that strained across his ample belly. He was forever coming over and asking if he could bring me things.

'Irene, would you like me to get you some

nylons?' he said one day. 'I know an American who can get me all sorts.'

Nylon tights were still in short supply in the UK and they were very expensive.

'Oh, no, Arthur, I don't think so,' I said.

But he refused to take no for an answer.

'They're lovely tights,' he said. 'So silky, and I can get them in all sorts of colours.'

In the end he badgered me so much I gave in.

'Oh, OK then,' I told him. 'I'll have some American tan, please.'

All the other girls were grinning and winking at me behind his back.

'What?' I said.

'I think Arthur's got a soft spot for you, Irene,' teased Peggy.

'Well, that's tough,' I said. 'I'm not in the least bit interested in him. I just want some nice tights.'

'But what's wrong with him?' asked Brenda.

'He just seems a bit dusty somehow,' I said. 'It must be all that time he spends in the orchestra pit.'

'Oh, Irene, you are funny,' she told me.

The next day Arthur came round to our dressing-room clutching a pair of nylons.

'Here you go, Irene,' he said, handing them to me.

'You were right,' I said. 'They are lovely and soft.'

'Irene, I just wondered whether you'd like to come out with me one Sunday when it's our day off,' he said.

'No, thank you, Arthur,' I said. 'I really don't want to go out with you, but can I still keep my tights?'

He looked disappointed. Even though I'd said no, he was very persistent and he was constantly asking me out.

'Are you sure you haven't changed your mind yet?' he'd say.

'I'm sure, Arthur,' I would sigh.

In the end the poor guy started to get quite depressed that I wouldn't go out with him.

'Oh, Irene, you're so mean,' Peggy told me. 'One date won't hurt you.'

'But he's not the least bit attractive and I don't want to string him along,' I said.

At least Arthur was a genuinely nice man. Unlike some blokes that we came across from time to time. One Sunday I was waiting at the bus stop to get a bus into town as we had rehearsals when a posh car pulled up and I saw a man waving at me. I realised it was the father of one of the young men who worked in the Palladium office. I'd seen him around the theatre a couple of times as he was also friendly with the management. He was a Russian man in his fifties.

'Hallo, darlink,' he said in his thick Russian accent. 'I recognise you from the vunderful

284

dancing girls at the Palladium. I'm heading there now and I vundered if you vanted a lift?'

It was Sunday, so I knew I could be waiting a while for a bus.

'That would be great,' I said, jumping in the front passenger seat. 'Thank you very much.'

He seemed a very respectable businessman in a suit and, judging by his car, he was obviously very wealthy.

'This is a very posh motor,' I said.

'Vhy thank you, Irene,' he said, putting his hand on my knee and giving it a pat. 'It is Irene, isn't it? I know my son has spoken of you and I remember your vunderful dancing.'

'That's very nice of you to say so,' I said, smiling politely.

In my naïvety I assumed that he was simply being friendly.

'I've just got to call in at my flat,' he said as we drove into town. 'It's only in Mayfair. I have remembered some important business documents that I need to take into the theatre today.'

'Oh, OK then,' I said.

We pulled up outside a grand Georgian building in a pretty square.

'Vould you like to come een with me, Irene, and have a look around?' he said.

'Well, I really should be getting to rehearsals,' I said, glancing at my watch.

'It vill only take five minutes,' he said.

'Oh, OK then,' I replied.

I followed him into the grand entrance hall with its huge crystal chandelier and marble floor.

'I hope your wife doesn't mind me disturbing her on a Sunday,' I said.

'Aaah no, my vife is back in Russia seeing her mother,' he said.

'Sit down,' he said, pointing to a leather Chesterfield. 'Would you like a drink?'

'Oh, no thank you,' I said. 'Not when I've got to work. I'll forget all my routines if I have a gin.'

I was surprised when he came and sat down beside me, and even more so when he put his hand on my knee. Suddenly I came to my senses. This was all a ploy to get me up to his apartment. How silly had I been? I jumped up from the settee.

'Don't you need to get your documents, then we can head to the theatre?' I said, slightly nervous now. 'Miss Doris and Miss Barbara both hate it if we're late for rehearsals and I'll get a telling off.'

'I vill be honest with you,' he said. 'There are no documents. I like you, Irene, and I vundered if you would consider going to bed vith me?'

I wasn't shocked or scared, I was just furious that he'd tricked me into going up there and I'd fallen for it hook, line and sinker.

'No, I will not sleep with you,' I said. 'I can't believe you brought me up here to proposition me. Now please take me to the Palladium, otherwise I will walk there myself.'

To give him his due, he was very apologetic.

'I'm sorry if I say the vong thing to you,' he said. 'But I like you very much. Please forgive me and please don't mention this to my son.'

'I won't,' I said. 'Now please let's go as I'm going to get such a telling off if I'm late.'

We drove to the Palladium in silence. I was cross with myself for being so naïve and shocked that an elderly businessman had propositioned me in broad daylight on a Sunday morning.

I got to the Palladium in the nick of time and jumped out of his car without saying another word.

'You won't believe what's just happened to me,' I said to Jean.

Her eyes were as wide as saucers as I described how the Russian had tried to seduce me at his flat.

'I'm just lucky that I managed to get out of there in one piece,' I said. 'Don't tell anyone else, though. I'm really embarrassed.'

'My lips are sealed,' said Jean. 'I hate the way that some men assume that because you're a dancer then you must have loose morals.'

Thankfully I never saw the Russian man around the Palladium again, and my run-in with him taught me not to be so trusting.

One by one the girls all met someone special. Jean eventually married her boyfriend Kenneth, Peggy started dating the flute player from the Skyrockets who she'd flirted with for years, and another girl, Lynn, married the manager of American performers Alice Faye and her husband Frankie Laine. They did a stint at the Palladium and were managed by Alice's brother, who swept Lynn off her feet, and she left to go and live in America. But most girls stayed in the Tillers even after they got married. If their husband wasn't in the same business then they would be more likely to leave, as stupidly some men were jealous at the thought of their wives being a dancer and being looked at by other blokes.

Not all their marriages were happy, though. Jean got pregnant soon after she married Kenneth and I was really sad to see her leave the Tillers. I went round to visit her one day at her new house in Essex when she was eight months pregnant. She opened the door and I was shocked to see that she had a black eye.

'Oh, Jean,' I said. 'What have you done? Don't tell me you've had a fall in your condition.'

She stared at the floor and wouldn't look at me.

'What is it?' I asked.

'Kenneth did it,' she said.

'You what?' I gasped, completely astonished.

'He just lost his rag and hit me,' she said. 'But it was my fault. I'd fallen asleep and forgotten about his dinner in the oven, and it was all burned.'

'Oh, Jean, you can't stay married to someone who does that to you,' I said. 'Especially when you're about to drop.'

'But he loves me, Irene, and he said sorry afterwards,' she told me. 'He just gets angry sometimes. Please don't tell anyone, will you?'

Domestic violence wasn't talked about in those days. In fact it didn't even have a name but was just seen as something that you had to put up with. There was no such thing as a refuge then, or anywhere safe for women to go. No one batted an eyelid if a husband gave his wife a good clip round the ear; that was just part and parcel of married life in the Fifties. But I knew I could never be married to someone who hit me.

'For God's sake, Jean,' I said. 'Why don't you come and stay with me in Battersea for a while?'

'I can't do that,' she said. 'I couldn't be on my own with a baby and no husband.'

We were both nervous when halfway through my visit Kenneth came home from work for his lunch. As soon as I saw him I knew I couldn't hold my tongue.

'I can't believe you hit a pregnant woman,' I told him. 'How could you do that to your own wife?'

'Irene, please don't,' begged Jean. 'Please don't make a scene.'

'I can't sit here and not say anything,' I said. 'I think it's disgusting and you should be ashamed of yourself.'

Kenneth didn't say a word. He looked shocked that a woman had spoken like that to him and he obviously didn't know what to say to me.

'I'm not frightened of you,' I told him. 'You need to keep your hands to yourself in future.'

I felt so bad for Jean. She was such a lovely, sweet girl and I hated to think of her married to a nasty piece of work like Kenneth. It was so frustrating. She was potty about him and that meant she would forgive him for anything, including hitting her.

That certainly didn't do anything to change my mind about men. As far as I could see they were just not worth the bother. I had my dancing and the theatre in my life; these were my passions and I didn't need anything or anyone else. No man would ever match up to that.

17

The Final Curtain

Even though it was Sunday and my day off from the Palladium I often did a bit of babysitting to make some extra money on the side.

One weekend I was babysitting for Antony Holland and his wife Gusta. He was an actor and she was a secretary, and in the daytime while they were at work I was looking after their two children – Roisin, who was seven, and Nelson, who was five – at their house in Shepherd's Bush.

'Just to let you know, Irene, Antony's younger brother Kaye, who's in the merchant navy, is due back at some point today,' said Gusta. 'I've told him you'll be here, so just let him in and tell him that we'll see him later.'

'No problem,' I said.

Later that afternoon there was a knock at the door and I opened it to find a young man standing there. He was very handsome, with thick, jet-black hair and dark eyes, and was wearing a knitted fisherman's jumper and jeans, which had just come to the UK from America and were very fashionable.

His face lit up into a huge smile when he saw me.

'My brother said there would be someone to let me in when I got here but I wasn't expecting a lovely young lady like you,' he said.

'I'm assuming you're Kaye,' I laughed. 'Come in.'

He told me he was a captain's steward in the merchant navy and had just come back from Australia.

'Gosh, that's a long way,' I said. 'What was it like there?'

'It was very hot and there were lots of kangaroos,' he told me.

We chatted for a couple of hours until Antony came home.

'Ah, I see you met Irene,' he said to Kaye, raising an eyebrow at him. 'I told Gusta that I thought you two would get along.'

'Yes,' he said. 'It was a nice surprise.'

I went to get my coat as I was due to catch the bus home from Shepherd's Bush to Clapham.

'Lovely to meet you, then,' I said to Kaye. 'Enjoy your time at home.'

'Wait a minute,' he said, running out of the door after me. 'It's late. Let me walk you to the bus stop.'

'Oh, only if you're sure,' I said.

We chatted all the way there and Kaye explained that he was back for two months before his next posting.

'Would you like to go out with me one night?' he asked.

'No, I don't think so,' I said. 'I work awkward hours, you see.'

'What do you do?' he asked.

'I'm a Tiller Girl and I dance at the Palladium,' I told him.

'Oh, that's unusual,' he said, looking a bit surprised. 'I've never met a dancer before. I know. Why don't I come to the Palladium and meet you after work tomorrow?'

He didn't seem to be put off by the fact I worked late, so we arranged to meet by the stage door after the show had finished.

I could tell he was keen on me and we'd got along well, so I thought it would be nice to see him again. The next evening, as I was taking my make-up off after the show, I was quite surprised by how excited and nervous I was.

'Don't tell anyone but I've met someone,' I told Peggy in the dressing-room. 'He's coming to see me tonight.'

'That's great, Irene,' she said. 'How exciting!'

'It might not lead to anything but he seems nice.'

I was last out of the stage door as usual, but when I came rushing out Kaye was nowhere to be seen.

'You looking for someone, Irene?' said

George the doorman.

'I'm supposed to be meeting someone,' I said. 'I'm sure he'll be here in a minute.'

'Oh, a "he", is it?' he said, raising his eyebrows. 'I see.'

'Oh, give over, George,' I laughed.

No one could keep anything to themselves at the Palladium.

I wasn't worried that I'd been stood up. I could tell Kaye liked me, so I knew he'd turn up eventually. But I was waiting half an hour before he came puffing down Argyll Street.

'There you are,' I said. 'About time and all.'

Kaye was in a right state. He was out of breath and sweat was dripping down his forehead.

'Sorry, Irene,' he panted. 'I went to the London Pavilion instead of the London Palladium.'

The poor beggar had rushed like hell from Leicester Square to Oxford Circus.

'You silly thing,' I said. 'Well, it doesn't matter, you're here now.'

When he'd got his breath back we went for a drink in the Argyll Arms, where the Skyrockets used to go between acts. We chatted away for ages and Kaye was easy company. He was very happy-go-lucky and he had a good sense of humour. He was quite political, and thankfully left-wing like me, so we shared similar views about things.

I checked my watch and suddenly got a bit of a shock.

'Oh, I'd better go or I'll miss the last Tube,' I said, drinking up my gin and tonic.

'I'll come with you and make sure you get home safely,' he said.

'That's very kind of you but really there's no need,' I told him. 'Clapham's nowhere near Shepherd's Bush.'

But Kaye was insistent and when we got to Clapham South station he even walked me right to my front door.

'Thank you for a lovely evening,' he said, giving me a peck on the cheek. 'Do you think I could come and meet you after work tomorrow night?'

'All right,' I said.

It was nearly midnight by then and the poor bloke had missed the last Tube, so he had to walk all the way home to Shepherd's Bush. It must have taken him hours.

That night I went to bed smiling. I wasn't a soppy, romantic person who wanted everything to be hearts and flowers, but Kaye was the first man that I'd met whom I had any interest in. The conversation flowed quite naturally between us and we just got along.

The following night I told all the girls about Kaye and how I was meeting him later.

'Ooh, Irene, can we see him?' asked Sylvia.

'If you want,' I told her.

I knew they were all going to have a good gawp no matter what I said. Kaye was obviously determined to be on time that evening and when I came out of the stage door he was already there, chatting to a few of the girls.

'Here she is,' said George. 'I told you she was always last out.'

Peggy gave me a nudge.

'He's lovely, Irene,' she whispered. 'A real catch.'

Every night that week Kaye met me after work. All the girls quickly got to know him, and they would file past and give him a peck on the way out, which always made his day.

On Sunday it was my day off so we arranged to go for a walk in Kew Gardens. We were sauntering along chatting when Kaye suddenly sank down onto the ground. I was shocked, thinking he'd keeled over.

'Kaye?' I said. 'What's the matter? Are you all right?'

Then he smiled and I realised that he was down on one knee. Oh, God, I thought, what the heck was he doing?

'Irene, will you do me the honour of being my wife?' he said, grabbing my hand.

'Don't be so stupid,' I said, dying of embarrassment as people walking past stopped and stared at us. 'We only met a week ago, I hardly know you.'

I knew he was half joking, but I could tell

there was a part of him that was serious too. I liked him an awful lot but it was far too early to even think about marriage. After all he was the first man that I'd ever really gone out with.

But as the weeks passed, I slowly found myself falling for him. We shared the same sense of humour and he made me laugh. We got on well as good friends, and he liked the fact that I had a strong opinion about things.

'That's great, Irene,' Brenda told me when we were chatting about it. 'Most men expect a woman to shut up and agree with everything they say.'

'I could never go out with someone like that who thinks their word is law,' I said.

Kaye encouraged me to speak my mind if I didn't agree with something. Like my views about war and how I didn't think it solved anything, which I was even more sure about having seen the injured soldiers here and the devastation in Germany.

I'd always thought, like a lot of the other girls, that I'd meet someone at the Palladium, as we spent most of our time there. But it didn't even cross my mind that Kaye wasn't in the theatre business. We had enough in common and I was fascinated by the fact that he was a sailor on the high seas. He was very well travelled and I loved hearing about all the places that he'd been.

One night, when we'd been seeing each

297

other a month or so, I got him tickets to come and see the show.

'I think it's about time that you came to see me dance,' I told him.

'I've never watched a variety show before,' he said.

As I got ready in the dressing-room that evening I started to feel a bit nervous.

'Kaye's out there watching tonight,' I told Peggy as I blobbed the hot black onto my eyelashes. 'I really hope he enjoys it.'

I was worried about what he was going to think, especially as he'd never seen anything like it before so he'd nothing to compare it with.

'I know some girls' boyfriends go all jealous and silly about them being a dancer and performing for other men,' I said.

'Shift over,' said Peggy, as she came and sat next to me in front of the mirror and started doing her lipstick. 'You've got nothing to worry about. Your Kaye's not like that. You said he likes the fact you've got your own career and opinions.'

'That's true,' I said. 'He does.'

I knew all that, but it still didn't stop me from worrying. I really wanted him to love it as much as I did, as dancing was such an important part of my life. In many ways it was my life – what if he didn't 'get it'?

'Come on, dolly daydream,' laughed Sylvia. 'We're all waiting for you here. It's time

298

to go down.'

'Oh, sorry, I didn't hear the call boy,' I said, quickly stepping into my shoes and following the rest of the girls down the stairs.

In a way Kaye had picked a good night to come. As well as doing our normal kicking routine in the line, we were doing a speciality waltz number with the star of the show, Gracie Fields. The stage had been set up to look like a ballroom, and instead of our usual short costumes we were wearing long white crinoline dresses and hats. We all had male dance partners who had been brought in specially for that performance and, as Gracie sang *The Girl in the Alice Blue Gown*, we all waltzed elegantly around the stage. As part of a Tiller troupe you were expected to turn your hand to any sort of routine at a moment's notice. But we ended the whole show with our usual high-energy, high-kicking number and, as I danced, I thought of Kaye out there in the second row of the audience and hoped he was enjoying it.

Afterwards he came backstage.

'Well?' I said nervously. 'What did you think?'

'I thought it was marvellous and you looked so glamorous,' he said.

'You were the best-looking one up there,' he told me, giving me a tender kiss on the cheek.

'Oh, thank you,' I said.

I wasn't used to being praised and it felt nice to be complimented, but also quite strange at the same time.

Kaye even met Miss Barbara and Miss Doris, who had slipped into the audience that night as they often did to check that our performance was up to scratch.

'Hello, dear,' said Miss Doris, shaking his hand. 'So you're Irene's special friend, are you?'

'Er, yes, I suppose I am,' said Kaye, looking a bit embarrassed.

Thankfully they seemed to like him.

'Well done, you're respectable enough to go out with me,' I joked afterwards.

'Well, I'm very relieved to have passed the Tiller test,' he said.

By now I'd even told my mother about Kaye.

'There's someone I'd like you to meet,' I told her.

I thought she would be relieved that I had a boyfriend at long last at the age of 21, but she seemed shocked and a bit disappointed.

'I always hoped that you'd settle down with a musician or at least someone from the theatre, Rene,' she said. 'What about that nice cello player next door? You never gave that poor boy a chance.'

For years she had been trying to get me to go out with the young musician next door, and he had even invited me out on a date. But I wasn't interested.

'Mother, he's probably very nice but he's just so straight-laced and boring,' I said.

By the time Kaye's leave was almost up and he was due to go back to sea, we both knew that things were serious between us. I wanted him to meet my family, but I didn't want to make a big deal about it as we were both nervous, so I casually brought him home one Sunday. No one knew he was coming so they couldn't make a fuss.

'This is Kaye,' I said, introducing him to my grandparents.

My grandfather took to him straight away, not least because Kaye had brought him a bottle of wine that he'd got when his ship had docked in Spain. Even my grandmother was quite charming to him, but my mother was a harder nut to crack. I knew she was never going to welcome him with open arms as we'd always been so close, and I think it was hard for her to see me in a relationship. She was very polite to him, but I could see she was a bit on edge and nervous. Harry was away on tour, fortunately, otherwise he probably would have behaved like a sulky teenager. A few days later Kaye also met Raymond when he called round. Although they didn't have a thing in common work-wise, they were both very political and intelligent men who shared similar views, and thankfully they seemed to get on well.

Soon it was time for Kaye to go back to sea. He could pick and choose his routes, and this time he'd made sure that he was allocated a European route so he wouldn't be gone for too long. But he was still going to be away for two months.

'I'm going to miss you,' I told him as he set off for Tilbury docks in Essex.

'I love you, Irene,' he said.

'Me too,' I smiled.

Although I missed him, I liked my freedom and independence, so in a way it suited me having a boyfriend who was away at sea. There was no way of phoning him on the ship, but we wrote to each other every week.

All the same I was looking forward to him coming home, and I was so pleased when I came out of the stage door one night to find his smiling face waiting for me.

'You're back!' I said, flinging my arms around him. 'I didn't expect to see you until tomorrow.'

'Ah, well. I persuaded the Thames tugboat captain to take me ashore early as soon as we docked,' he said. 'I told him that I had to race to the Palladium and see my sweetheart.'

He'd come back with his kitbag full of things he'd bought in Europe – wine, cigarettes, butter, and a beautiful silk scarf for me.

This time he was home for a month before

he was due back at sea. Kaye's parents Edwin and Beatrice lived in Devon, where they ran a milk bar, and I went down and met them and his four older brothers.

Eventually we got used to being apart for months on end and enjoying the time that he had on leave when he got home. I was up north doing a summer season again when he arrived home next time. So he got the train up to see me for a few days. There was no way Kaye would ever be allowed to stay overnight at my grandparents' house, and he always stayed with Antony and Gusta when he was home, but when he was visiting me there he stayed in my room at the guest-house.

We were walking down the seafront arm in arm one day when Kaye turned to me and said: 'Shall we get engaged?'

I knew by then that we would get married one day.

'This time I think I'll say yes,' I smiled.

All my friends in the Tillers had started to get married and have children, and new girls had replaced them in the troupe.

Everybody had moved on with their lives, and I felt it was time for me to move on with my mine too. Kaye was the only man that I'd ever met that I could see myself doing that with.

We went straight to a jeweller's together to look at rings. 'The thing is, I don't really like brand new sparkly jewellery or big diamonds,' I told him.

'Well, that's fine by me,' said Kaye.

So we went to a little second-hand shop where I saw an opal ring surrounded by a circle of tiny diamonds that cost £20. 'It's perfect,' I said.

The other girls in the show were so happy for me, but I think our wardrobe mistress Jim was the most excited. When he saw my ring he let out a loud, high-pitched screech.

'Oh, Irene, I'm delighted for you,' he said, giving me a big hug.

I couldn't wait to tell my mother the news, so before that night's show I rushed to a phone box in town.

'Guess what, Mum?' I said. 'Kaye and I have got engaged.'

'Oh,' she said.

'Aren't you happy for me?' I asked her.

'Yes, dear, of course I am,' she said.

But she didn't really say very much and I could tell by the tone of her voice that she was upset. I think part of her was sad at the thought of me leaving home and starting my own family. I think Mum had struggled so much financially after my father died that if I couldn't marry a musician then she probably wanted me to be with someone who had plenty of money and could give me financial security. Kaye certainly wasn't that person, but I wasn't getting married for money.

We didn't get married for several months, as there was never a time that Kaye was home and I wasn't working, but finally we set the date for a Saturday in March 1952, a couple of months before I turned twenty-two.

Neither of us wanted a big do, and it wasn't really the norm in those days to have a huge fancy wedding as we were still in the austere times after the war. We weren't religious so we booked Battersea Register Office for the ceremony, and I bought a long-sleeved grey suit from the West End and a very fashionable lime green hat and black high heels.

My mother and grandparents came, as did Kaye's mother, my brother Raymond, his wife Evelyn and a handful of Tiller Girls. Harry was away working so he wasn't there.

'You look beautiful, Irene,' said Peggy, throwing rice over me as we came down the steps. It was traditional to throw rice at newlyweds in those days – it stemmed back to olden times when grains like wheat and rice were seen as symbols of fertility and prosperity.

Afterwards we all went back to my grand-parents' house for a glass of sherry or a cup of tea. My mother had done some chicken sandwiches and a kindly neighbour had made us a wedding cake. It was all over in a couple of hours.

'Well, I guess it's time for our honeymoon,

Mrs Holland,' laughed Kaye.

We'd splashed out on one night at the Ritz as I was due back at work at the Palladium the following day to rehearse for a new American variety season. We could only afford one of the smallest rooms right on the top floor of the hotel but it still seemed so grand to me. I couldn't believe it the next day when we had croissants and jam for breakfast. I'd never seen a croissant before in my life and I felt very sophisticated tucking into one of those.

I walked straight from Green Park to the Palladium for 9 a.m.

'Here comes the blushing bride,' teased Jack the stage manager when he saw me.

All the backstage crew wished me all the best, although the Skyrockets teased me something chronic.

'Here's the little wife,' one of them said. 'Don't you have to go home and make your new husband dinner?'

They knew exactly how to rattle my cage, but I just laughed it off.

'He knows he can make his own dinner,' I said.

A couple of weeks after the wedding Kaye and I moved into our own place in Tooting. It was a first-floor Victorian flat with big bay windows. I knew how to cook from watching my mother, but I'd never really had to before because I mainly ate out at cafés in between shows. But it was quite a novelty playing house, buying a recipe book and cooking lunch for my new husband before I left for the theatre. It was never anything fancy, just sausage and mash or roasts, but I wanted to do it when he was home as it made me feel like a proper grown-up.

Even though I was never bothered about having a boyfriend, the one thing I had been sure about all my life was that I wanted to be a mother. I just loved children and I always wanted to have a big family of my own. But with Kaye working away a lot of the time, it was a year before I fell pregnant.

He was back at sea by the time I found out, so I wrote to him to tell him the good news.

'Congratulations, you're going to be a daddy!' I wrote.

He was over the moon.

I was really happy and excited that I was going to be a mother, but I knew that it meant I would have to leave the Tiller Girls and the Palladium. I could only dance for the first few months, as the doctor wouldn't allow it after that and I wouldn't be able to fit into my costumes any more.

I also had to tell Miss Barbara and Miss Doris.

'I just wanted to let you know that I'm expecting a baby,' I said.

'Well, that's lovely, dear,' smiled Miss

Doris. 'We'll be sorry to lose you after all this time though, Irene.'

In a way I'd timed things perfectly, as the current American variety season was due to end when I was around three months pregnant. I was happy to keep on dancing for as long as possible, as luckily I didn't feel overly tired or have any morning sickness. But the last show came around all too soon for my liking. In what was perhaps a fitting end to my career as a Tiller Girl, one of the dances in the final show was a ballet number on pointe. We were all wearing pink ballet dresses with satin bodices, a heart-shaped neckline and frilly bits of chiffon on the shoulder straps. The top came to a point at the front, and then there was a calf-length skirt made out of four or five layers of net. They were beautiful, but as I'd put on a few pounds in my first few weeks of pregnancy mine proved to be a bit on the snug side!

'This is a bit of a squeeze, Irene,' laughed Peggy, as she struggled to do up the hooks and eyes on the back of my evening dress.

But instead of gliding about as in a normal ballet, we were going to do the routine in our line on the front cloth of the stage with the curtains closed behind us. It felt strange hearing the Skyrockets playing a slower, more sedate number, and in a way it matched my reflective mood. As we took up our usual positions in the line and all rose up onto pointe at the same time, I felt such a mixture of emotions. I was so looking forward to being a mum and excited about having a baby, but at the same time I felt so sad to be leaving my old life and the Palladium behind. I loved my freedom and my independence, and most of all I loved working at the world's most famous theatre, hearing the roar of the crowd and ending every show with a terrific buzz. God, I was going to miss it.

Our final dance to close the show, the season and my last performance as a Tiller Girl was our usual high-kicking routine. I knew all the different steps so well by now I could practically do them in my sleep. It was effortless and I didn't need to think about it; it was as instinctive to me as breathing. Even though I'd danced so many times on that stage it had never, ever felt mundane to me and I had enjoyed every single second. I would never tire of it. Never before had I danced there feeling sad, but as I high-kicked my way off to the side of the stage and the curtain fell for the final time, I realised that I had tears in my eyes.

'Are you all right, Irene?' asked Sylvia.

I nodded.

'It just feels like the end of an era for me,' I said. 'I know that I'll dance again at some point, but it won't be as a Tiller and it won't be here.'

God knows how many times I'd danced on

that stage over the past four years, the routines I'd learnt, the costumes I'd worn and all the amazing stars I'd met. It had been one heck of an experience and one I knew I would never forget as long as I lived.

We all ran back up to the dressing-room and I took my make-up off with paraffin and left my rags on the side for the last time – all the little rituals I'd performed without thinking for six nights a week over the years. All the girls came over to say goodbye to me before they left.

'I'm going to miss this place,' I sighed, giving them all a hug.

All the old faces that I'd started with more than four years ago had gone now, except Peggy and Sylvia.

'We're going to miss you, Irene,' said Peggy. 'The troupe won't be the same without you.'

She was due to be married herself in a couple of months.

'It's time for me to move on with my life,' I said.

'Keep in touch,' said Sylvia.

'I'll try,' I said.

But I knew it didn't work like that. Everyone was busy with husbands and new babies, and those who still danced travelled all over the country for work and were seldom at home. Even with girls you'd known well for years you tended to lose touch eventually when you stopped working together.

I looked around the now empty dressing-room and smiled. As usual I was the last to leave. I thought about how much I had changed from that naïve seventeen-year-old who had first danced for Miss Barbara and Miss Doris. During that time I had done so much and met so many different people, from injured servicemen to huge Hollywood stars. And I had met Kaye, fallen in love and now I was going to be a mother. That was going to be my new challenge and I was determined that I was going to give it my all, as I did with everything in my life.

Slowly I started to pack up my things. I put all of my stage make-up into my box – the carmine that was slowly being replaced by rouge, my red lipsticks and the hot black. Some of the newer girls were now using false eyelashes, which had started to become more readily available, as well as nylon stockings instead of white wet, although these were still very expensive. I packed up all my shoes – my ballet, tap and pointe shoes, and my black Cuban-heeled pair.

I mustn't forget my autograph books, I told myself, as I searched under my bench for the two huge books containing the signatures of all the stars whom I had worked with over the years.

Seeing the dressing-room empty like this, I realised how shabby it was. There was dust and cobwebs everywhere, the wooden furniture was scratched and battered, the floor was scuffed, and the walls were damp and bare. But it didn't matter. I knew every musty nook and cranny of this place like the back of my hand, and it had been like home to me. I picked up my big, heavy bag, and as I walked down the steep, stone staircase for the last time I couldn't bring myself to look back.

There was something so special about the Palladium and I had nothing but happy memories of working there.

'Bye, George,' I said to the doorman.

'Good luck with the baby, Irene,' he said. 'You'll make him or her a lovely mother.'

'Thank you,' I said. 'You look after yourself.'

Then I closed the stage door behind me and left the Palladium for the last time, knowing that I'd never be a Tiller Girl again.

18

New Beginnings

The pains were coming thick and fast now, and I was bent double, gripping onto the side of the settee.

'It's getting worse,' I told my mother through gritted teeth.

'Hang on, dear, and I'll phone you a taxi,' she said.

I was in labour with my first child, who was a week overdue. Kaye was away at sea and so I got a taxi to the South London Hospital for Women and Children on my own. Thankfully it was only up at Clapham Common so I didn't have far to go.

I was frightened to death and there was no one with me to reassure me, but that was the norm in those days. It wasn't the done thing to have your mother at a hospital birth. If a husband did come to the hospital he would pace around in the waiting-room smoking cigars, but most men waited in the pub and started to wet the baby's head well in advance.

It was a long, hard labour and I was exhausted.

'Your muscles are so tight that your body won't relax and let that baby out,' the nurse told me.

Finally, after twenty-six hours, my son Barry was born and it was such a relief.

The sister came over to me just after I'd given birth.

'I need some information for this form,' she said. 'What's your religion?'

'None,' I said.

'None?' she gasped. 'What do you mean?'

'I mean I don't believe in anything,' I told her.

'Well, I can't possibly put that down,' she said.

We ended up having an argument because she point-blank refused to believe that I didn't belong to any religion.

In those days new mothers stayed in hospital for a week to convalesce. Mum came to see me and she was delighted to be a grandmother.

'Oh, Rene, he's beautiful,' she said.

'Can you let Kaye know for me?' I asked her.

So she sent a telegram to his ship.

You're the father of a baby boy, she wrote.

We'd had to give up the lease on our flat in Tooting as babies weren't allowed there, so I'd moved back in with my mother and grandparents in Battersea. But not everyone was happy about that decision. The day I left hospital I walked into the living-room holding Barry, and Harry gave me a look of utter disdain.

'I'm not staying in this house with that baby here,' he told Mum. 'You're going to make more of a fuss of him than you do of me. I can't stand to sit here and watch you cooing over him.' He got up and walked out, and Mum burst into tears.

I was furious with him.

'He's the one behaving like a baby,' I said.

I thought it was pathetic. Mum managed to persuade him to come back, but I knew it would cause problems if we stayed there for too long. When Kaye came back on leave I sat him down.

'We can't stay here,' I said. 'Things are really awkward with Harry, and my poor mother's stuck in the middle.'

But I knew we couldn't really afford to rent much in London, never mind buy our own place.

'Why don't we move to Devon?' said Kaye. 'In Tiverton we'll be near my parents and things are so much cheaper down there. It's a lovely place to bring up a family.'

I'd only ever been to Devon a couple of times and I hardly knew anything about it, but it would be a new adventure.

'OK then,' I said. 'Let's give it a go.'

Mum was devastated when I said I was leaving London.

'What do you want to go to Devon for?' she said. 'It's all fields and cows.'

'It will be a new start and eventually we might be able to afford to buy a place down there.'

'Rene, get your head out of the clouds,' she said. 'It's very different to London, and it's not going to be all white picket fences and roses, you know.'

Mum was right. To say it was a culture shock was an understatement. I was a city girl and I loved the buzz of London. I missed the hustle and bustle of all the people, the shops, the Tubes and buses – and, of course, the theatres. I'd never been one for going on long country walks or wading through muddy fields in wellingtons and I was like a fish out of water. I went into town one day and people stared at me as if I were an alien. I still dressed the way I did when I lived in London, as that was me.

'Just because I'm living in the country now doesn't mean that I can't make an effort,' I told Kaye.

I was all dolled up in high heels, big gold earrings and bright red lipstick, pushing Barry along the high street in his pram.

'I can tell you're not from round 'ere with that cockney accent,' said a man in a shop. 'You're Kaye's wife, ain't yarr?'

'Yes,' I said, although I was desperate to point out that I had a London accent and not a cockney one.

I think stupidly I thought I'd fit in right away, but it took time to make friends and feel at home. Soon I was pregnant again, and Kaye's father Edwin helped us with the deposit to buy a big Victorian house that needed renovating. And then things got even tougher. I was stuck in a run-down house with a baby in a strange town while Kaye was away for weeks on end and I was struggling to cope. When Barry got bronchial pneumonia, I hit breaking point. I was exhausted as he wasn't sleeping and he had a dan-

316

gerously high temperature. The house was so drafty, and I had to keep him in his crib in the kitchen as that was the warmest room. I was really anxious dealing with it on my own. After my second son Trevor was born I got very tired and depressed.

When Kaye came home on leave I told him: 'I don't think I can do this on my own any more. I don't think I can cope.'

So he decided to leave the merchant navy, stay at home and help to run the family's milk bar, which was wonderful and made life quite a bit easier.

I loved being a mother and I went on to have my third son Raymond, but I still just didn't feel like me any more. In my heart I was always a dancer.

If someone asked me, 'What do you do?' I'd always reply, 'I'm a dancer.'

I'd not danced since I'd left the Palladium, and I was too busy and tired learning how to be a mother to be a dancer now. Then one day there was a knock at the door.

It was a woman, who had with her a little girl of about five.

'Are you Irene Holland?' she asked.

'Yes.'

'I heard you used to be a dancer in London and I wondered if you'd be able to teach my little girl Margaret ballet?' she said. 'She's desperate to learn.'

'Oh,' I said. 'I'm not really sure. I've never

taught before.'

But I felt bad turning her away.

'Why don't you bring her round after school tomorrow and I'll give it a go?' I told her.

So while two of the boys were sleeping and Raymond was in his baby chair I gave her a lesson in the front room.

'Right, then,' I said, as she stood in the middle of the room. 'We'd better get started.'

I think we were both as nervous as each other. First of all I put *Swan Lake* on the record-player, and as soon as I heard the music all of my early training suddenly came flooding back to me and I knew exactly what to do. It was both a surprise and a relief as I hadn't had time to plan a lesson or even make any notes.

I started off by showing her first position.

'Stand nice and tall with your heels together and your feet turned out,' I said, showing her what I meant.

Then I got her to rise up on her demi-pointes, which is where you go up high on the balls of your feet.

'That's lovely, dear,' I said. 'Pretend you're a flower and keep growing up tall. Keep your bottom in and your chest up and your neck nice and long like a swan.'

All of the things that Miss Moira and Miss Toni had taught me all those years ago came back to me in an instant, and I remembered how much joy and satisfaction I'd felt in ballet class when I'd mastered pliés and pointes. I'd had such good training that I think it had become second nature to me, like riding a bike or cleaning my teeth. I could remember everything that I'd learned at Italia Conti all those years ago. Before I knew it the hour was up.

'Aw, have we finished already?' Margaret said.

'Yes, dear,' I told her. 'Would you like to have another lesson?'

She nodded her head eagerly.

'Thank you,' I told her mum afterwards. 'I really enjoyed that.'

'She liked it too,' she told me. 'Can she come again next week and could she bring her friend Janet with her?'

'Yes,' I said. 'I don't see why not.'

Although I'd never really thought about teaching before, I realised that I'd loved every minute of it. There was a real satisfaction in passing knowledge and seeing a child passionate about dance.

Word soon spread, and over the next few weeks I had more and more people coming to the front door.

'Could you teach my daughter ballet?'

'My son's desperate to learn tap.'

I soon had a class of ten children all learning ballet in my front room once a week.

'I'm going to have to teach tap in the

kitchen as the floor's stone in there and much harder,' I told Kaye.

Then my father-in-law Edwin had an idea.

'I know, Irene,' he said. 'Why don't I help you turn the front room into a proper dance studio?'

So he painted the floor black and put a ballet barre down one side, and I bought a second-hand record-player to play my music on.

By then I'd fallen pregnant again with my fourth child but I was determined to carry on. When I was teaching I felt like me again and I started to really love it. I got such a kick from seeing the children enjoy them-selves and learn to love dancing like I did. For me the thrill of teaching replaced the buzz of performing on the stage.

'I can't wait until my class next week,' a little girl told me on her way out one evening.

'You know, that's the best praise anyone could ever give me,' I said.

But soon I had so many children wanting lessons that I couldn't fit them all into my cramped front room, so I decided to start my own dance school. One night a week I hired a village hall and Kaye looked after the children while I taught three hours of classes.

I also started a little dance troupe of six teenage girls and we put on shows for charity in local clubs. I loved working out the choreography and doing the costumes.

Kaye and I were also well on the way to creating our own dance troupe at home. I went on to have three daughters – Diana, Nancy and Nina – and we also adopted a little girl called Rosalind. My mother was absolutely horrified whenever I got pregnant again.

'I've always wanted a big family,' I told her, but she just didn't get it. The idea of having seven children was completely alien to her.

'I just wanted something different for you, Rene,' she said.

As the dance school continued to grow I couldn't handle it all on my own any more and I took on some teachers. I was what was known as a professional teacher – someone who's been in the business. I also went to college and got a teacher's certificate.

I never pushed my own children into liking dance, but they followed me round like little ducks, and they were all interested in coming to my classes and performing in my troupes. They all tried it and loved it, and I think I was secretly pleased when, one by one, they all said, 'Mummy, I want to dance.'

I never expected any of them to do it as a career, but five out of the seven of them have danced professionally. Raymond went to the Nesta Brooking School of Ballet and the

London School of Contemporary Dance, and he's appeared in five West End musicals. Diana studied ballet at Nesta Brooking too and has danced around the world. Nancy runs her own theatre school in New Zealand, and both Barry and Ros went to the London School of Contemporary Dance. Nina has a lovely singing voice and has appeared in lots of my productions.

In 1986 Raymond won the role of one of the lead dancers in *La Cage aux Folles*.

'Mum, it's on at the Palladium,' he said and he invited Kaye and me to the opening night to watch it.

I was excited and so proud to see him, but I was also thrilled about going back to the Palladium. I hadn't been back for thirty-four years, not since the day I'd left, but as I walked into the foyer and saw the huge sweeping staircase and all the red and gold it felt so familiar.

'It's just like coming home,' I said to Kaye.

It was a brilliant show and I loved every minute of it. Being at the Palladium brought back so many happy memories. I very rarely sat in the audience when I worked there, apart from during rehearsals, so it was a real treat. It still had the same energy and special atmosphere that it always had. Afterwards I was invited backstage and I knew it like the back of my hand.

'It's all exactly the same,' I said.

All of the people whom I'd worked with all those years ago had long gone, but from the dressing-rooms up in the attic to the stage door absolutely nothing else in the building had changed. It seemed so long since I'd sat at that mirror, doing my make-up and chatting to the other girls. I knew I couldn't dance like the young woman that I used to be when I performed there, but it no longer mattered.

Teaching had become my new love. It was lovely to watch people become competent dancers and to see how happy doing one of my classes made them feel, because I remembered feeling exactly the same.

I loved seeing the way that dancing made shy, introverted or troubled children come out of their shell and flourish. It's not about failure or being the best dancer, and it doesn't matter if they don't want to dance professionally; for me it has always been about the joy that dancing can bring.

One day, a few years ago, there was a knock at my door. I opened it to find a young lad I knew of called Jason. He only lived around the corner from me in Tiverton and he was nineteen.

'I want to learn how to dance and I wondered if you could help me,' he said.

He explained that he'd wanted to be a professional dancer all his life but he'd been terrified of doing anything about it in case people laughed at him. I could tell that he had a burning desire to dance that had suddenly erupted inside him.

In all honesty I knew he'd left it quite late in his life if he wanted to dance professionally, but I didn't say that. I will never turn anyone away. Anyone can come to my classes as long as they are prepared to work.

'OK, then,' I said. 'I'll teach you to dance on one condition.'

'What's that, then?' he asked.

'If you take that ring out of your nose and the one out of your lip because I don't like it.'

'OK, Mrs Holland,' he smiled.

So Jason started coming to my ballet classes once a week, and after a few months I was stunned. He instantly took to classical dance and he had an incredible talent. It was as if he were born to do it.

I taught him ballet for three years and I was so pleased for him when he won a funded place at ballet school.

'Thank you, Irene, you've changed my life,' he told me. 'If it wasn't for you giving me a chance then I never would have achieved my dream.'

'You did it,' I said. 'It's your achievement and talent that's got you here.'

He went on to perform all over the world and at the Royal Opera House in Covent Garden.

It's wonderful being able to impart my knowledge and skills to somebody else who didn't think that they could do it. It's like giving something back. I'm not being righteous, and I know it's a cliché, but there are rewards on both sides. It's like the story of the ugly duckling. There's nothing more satisfying than seeing the person you thought couldn't dance, or who didn't want to, suddenly turn into a swan and flourish right before your eyes. My aim is to bring the best out of each and every child. They don't have to be brilliant or want to be a professional dancer. I just want them to enjoy it.

Over the years there have been students who have excelled, and many of them have gone on to study at prestigious performing arts and ballet schools. These places used to be funded and people got grants, but that doesn't happen anymore. I've known parents who have taken out second mortgages on their houses so their child can go to stage school. It's all very wrong, as it means only the wealthier children can succeed. If that had happened in my day then I would never have become a dancer in the first place.

Then sometimes, years later, my pupils come back and start working with me. Many of my current teachers are ex-students and some of my first pupils are in their fifties now. It's gone full circle – I taught their children and now I'm teaching their grandchildren, which is lovely. I still remember my dance teachers all these years later. If they're good teachers, even if they're dragons like Toni Shanley, they give you something that you don't ever forget.

Sadly I don't know what happened to any of the other Tiller Girls whom I danced with at the Palladium. Over the years we all lost touch as we moved on with our lives, but I still have so many fond memories of that time. I'm very much a today person, and I don't look back or dwell on the past. I don't talk about my background, and most of the staff and children at the dance school don't know much about my early career.

Sometimes I'll be chatting to one of my teachers and I'll mention in passing that I worked with a certain star or performed at a particular theatre.

'Really, Irene,' they gasp. 'You never told us that.'

'Well, you never asked,' I say to them.

Most of the star names I worked with would mean nothing to my students today, and they don't know much about the Tiller Girls. But sometimes for fun I'll get them to do a kicking routine during class.

'This is like what I used to do when I was a Tiller Girl,' I tell them.

'Come on, Irene, do some high kicks for us,' they'll say, egging me on.

And I used to until a few years ago, but it's

too much like hard work to do more than a couple now I'm eighty-four.

'Are you trying to give me a heart attack?' I joke.

Sometimes I'll have a quick flick through my autograph book and I'm stunned by all the amazing, talented people whom I was lucky enough to work with all those years ago, but other than that, for me, it's always about what's next.

When I look back on my life I don't have any regrets. Mum died well into her eighties and she was still playing her violin right up until her death. She might not have given me praise as a child, but I always had the strong sense that she loved me dearly. What she did give me was my musical background. All my life I was surrounded by music and I still constantly play music today. I think that's helped so much with teaching and choreography. And she gave me the chance to pursue my passion – for that I can never thank her enough.

It was hard being criticised as a child by my grandparents and aunties and uncles, and always having the feeling I was being looked down on.

Before he died, my mum's brother, Uncle Arthur, said to me: 'Nobody really took any notice of how successful you were, Rene, and that was terrible.'

But I refused to feel bitter about it.

'Well, I'm glad you noticed it now,' I told him.

In my dance school I create an environment in which every child is made a fuss of because I wasn't when I was growing up. I like to give them praise and recognition because I know how important that is.

I've been running the Willow Tree Centre of Dance and Performing Arts for over fifty years now. I've got ten teachers and over 250 pupils, and we're based at the local high school. As well as running the business I still teach – and I wouldn't have it any other way. I teach the five- and six-year-olds ballet, which I love because they're so funny, and they can listen and respond to simple discipline.

'All dancers have got straight backs and they don't talk,' I tell them. 'Why don't we talk?'

'Because we can't hear the music, Irene,' they say.

'The conductor would be very cross with you if you talk, so you need to have extra-large ears to hear the music,' I tell them.

Over the years I've developed all these little tricks to get them to do what I want them to do without making them feel worried or nervous.

'Have you lit the stars up tonight?' I ask them. 'You're not going to see them on the way home if you haven't stood on your

328

tiptoes and lit them up.'

All I really want them to do is rise on their demi-pointes with straight knees, but if I put it like that they wouldn't understand what I was asking them to do.

And just like I was as a child, and in fact still am now, they're all obsessed with fairies. I get great joy from choreographing our annual shows and designing the costumes and, of course, I always make sure that there are a few fairies in there. Sometimes I'll ask the children in my class: 'Have any of you seen a fairy?'

'Yes, I have,' they tell me excitedly.

But there's always one who will say: 'But they're not real.'

'Haven't you been down to the bottom of the garden lately?' I tell this one. 'You're obviously not looking hard enough.'

They like that idea of a magical world, just like the pantomime fairies that sparked my love of dance when I was a child. To me, dance is a magical world.

I love being with the children as they're great fun. I get bored very easily and over the years I've tried taking up hobbies like sewing, painting and bingo, but they're not for me. Nothing gets me as excited as music and dance. I can't imagine ever doing anything else and I've got no intention of retiring just yet. Even if they have to push me into class in my wheelchair, I'll still be there! Kaye and I have been married for sixty-two years now and he knows how important dancing is to me. It is – and always will be – my big passion in life and my greatest love. It's who I am and what I live for, and to be able to pass that on to other people really does feel like a precious gift. Our dance school has a motto, which is a saying from the German philosopher Friedrich Nietzsche – 'Out of chaos comes a dancing star.' That sums it all up for me. The rest of your life can be a mess, or you can have problems you're struggling to deal with, but dance will always be an escape and bring you great joy. Music and dancing make people happy, and they've certainly kept me smiling. I just feel so very lucky to have been able to do what I love for so long.

Acknowledgements

I'd like to thank all of the fantastic teachers at the Italia Conti Academy of Theatre Arts. I loved every minute that I spent there. Thank you to all my wonderful teachers at the Willow Tree Dance Centre. I'd like to say thank you to all my special helpers, especially to my wonderful friend Trish Ashton, the chaperones, pianists, backstage crew and the wardrobe ladies, including Denise James, who has made some incredible costumes over the past thirty years. Thanks to all students, past and present. You're the reason that I want to keep on working and teaching. Many thanks to everyone involved in the production of this book – Vicky Eribo at HarperCollins, my literary agent Rowan Lawton, and my new friend and ghost-writer Heather Bishop, who has made it all such good fun. And a special thank you to Justin Dollie, my taxi driver, for getting me about and for making me laugh with your jokes.